DOING SOCIAL JUSTICE EDUCATION

DOING SOCIAL JUSTICE EDUCATION

A Practitioner's Guide for Workshops and Structured Conversations

D. Scott Tharp with Roger A. Moreano

Foreword by Rev. Dr. Jamie Washington

STERLING, VIRGINIA

Sty/us

COPYRIGHT © 2020 BY STYLUS PUBLISHING, LLC.

Published by Stylus Publishing, LLC.
22883 Quicksilver Drive
Sterling, Virginia 20166-2019

Library of Congress Cataloging-in-Publication Data
Names: Tharp, D. Scott, author. | Moreano, Roger A.,
author.
Title: Doing social justice education : a practitioner's
guide for
   workshops and structured conversations / D. Scott
Tharp with Roger A.
   Moreano ; Foreword by Rev. Dr. Jamie Washington.
Description: First edition. | Sterling, Virginia : Stylus
Publishing,
   [2020] | Includes bibliographical references and index.
Identifiers: LCCN 2020043525 | ISBN 9781642670370
(paperback) | ISBN
   9781642670363 (hardback) | ISBN 9781642670394
(ebook) | ISBN
   9781642670387 (pdf)
Subjects: LCSH: Social justice--Study and teaching. |
Educational
   equalization. | Educational sociology.
Classification: LCC LC192.2 .T46 2020 | DDC 306.43--
dc23
LC record available at https://lccn.loc.gov/2020043525

13-digit ISBN: 978-1-64267-036-3 (cloth)
13-digit ISBN: 978-1-64267-037-0 (paperback)
13-digit ISBN: 978-1-64267-038-7 (library networkable
e-edition)
13-digit ISBN: 978-1-64267-039-4 (consumer e-edition)

Printed in the United States of America

All first editions printed on acid-free paper
that meets the American National Standards Institute
Z39-48 Standard.

Bulk Purchases

Quantity discounts are available for use in
workshops and for staff development.
Call 1-800-232-0223

First Edition, 2020

To my partner, Krista, for helping me be the best version of myself. And to my son Leo, who I hope will contribute to a more socially just world.
—D. Scott Tharp

For Zoe, Zach, and Zandi, my everything; for Maria, my twin soul; and for my mamacita and papi who always reminded me to "siempre sigue adelante con su cabeza limpia."
—Roger A. Moreano

Contents

Foreword

"We need a diversity session for our student leaders, how much time do you need?"

"Why do we have to spend all day in another diversity workshop? I did that last semester"

"Does the diversity session always have to be led by people of color?"

"I saw this fun game we can use for diversity training; I think the RA's will like it."

Adams, Bell, and Griffin (2007) define *social justice* as both a process and a goal: "The goal of social justice education is full and equal participation of all groups in a society that is mutually shaped to meet their needs. Social justice includes a vision of society that is equitable, and all members are physically and psychologically safe and secure" (p. 1). The power of this definition rests in the second sentence. It is a vision, thus making it aspirational and something we have not yet achieved. It is also powerful that these scholars name social justice as both a process and a goal. This definition invites us to consider it's about not only achieving the vision but also how we achieve it.. The road we travel matters.

I am honored to share in this foreword my thoughts, feelings, and experiences with social justice education and why this book is so important and relevant at this time. Building on the work of Adams, Bell, and Giffin, and others, these authors invite us on a journey that focuses on the process of achieving social justice through doing social justice education.

In 1981, as a resident assistant (RA), I did what I would consider my first social justice workshop. I was an RA on an all-male floor at a small public state institution in western Pennsylvania. I had no clue what I was doing. I just knew it was important to do a program on diversity, so I decided to do something on sexual orientation. At that time, all we understood was that a person was either heterosexual or homosexual. There was some room for bisexuality, but it was not really understood as a real sexual orientation and

seen as more of a place holder as one tried to figure out who there really were. At no time did I consider how my being Black, straight passing, Christian, and male would affect this session. I had no foundational knowledge on how oppression worked or how socialization matters. I didn't know I needed to plan my session with learning outcomes. I just knew I needed to do something around diversity, and gays and lesbians were a population that experienced oppression, thus, sexual orientation seemed like a good place to start.

My story is not all that different from many of my contemporaries doing social justice education work in the 1980s. We didn't fully understand what it took to create experiences grounded in sound theoretical frameworks and that would guide the design and the delivery of these learning experiences.

The authors offer us a clear process on important elements of design, facilitation, and assessment of social justice workshops and structured conversations. The first thing I found striking was the distinction between workshops and structured conversations. Many practitioners conflate the two. Both of these processes are important pedagogical tools for social justice education; however, they are not the same things.

I would say that my first attempt as an RA in 1981 was a structured conversation not a workshop. I did not understand the importance of creating the space for authentic engagement nor did I consider how my identities would inform the ways the conversation might unfold. Given the increase in peer led social justice sessions, it is critically important that we prepare our student leaders to facilitate these conversations in ways that support our learning outcomes.

The creation of learning outcomes is the area that I feel many folks doing social justice work could improve. The passion to end oppression is often the driving force for many social justice activists who are performing the role of educator. However, being a social justice educator requires a capacity to engage beyond the core value of "liberty and justice for all." It requires an understanding of and a capacity to design curriculum, select activities, and engage in conversations that will support participant learning. These experiences must provide an opportunity for reflection, dissonance, insight, and application. They cannot be simply designed to give people more information about how oppression works and why it's wrong. Many folks struggle with participation in social justice education experiences because they are delivered poorly, not just out of resistance. The authors help us to see how important it is to be grounded in context, solid theoretical frameworks, sound pedagogical activities, and strong facilitation skills. These four areas are a recipe for success.

Additionally, the authors invite us to a culture of evidence. In a time when we need to justify every dime spent; in a time when we need to demonstrate the real value of higher education, social justice education programs must be able to demonstrate their contribution to the preparation of the next generation of leaders. Therefore, assessment is a necessity. The authors help us to get clear about the importance of assessment in social justice education. It is not simply participant satisfaction. Participants are often unsatisfied with learning about how they have benefited from or colluded with systemic oppression. That does not mean the training did not achieve its learning objectives. Asking the right questions in the right time frame will yield important results for the efficacy of our work.

Finally, the authors offer three examples of what doing this work looks like. These are important case studies that illustrate how to move from theory to practice. They allow us to consider lessons learned and how we might be able to tweak some of the processes and activities and give them a try on our campuses.

This project gives me great joy. Doing social justice education is my life. It is my calling. It is my activism. It is how I intend to leave the world better that I found it. This book will become a part of the cannon for the next generation of social justice educators and I'm grateful to be a part of it.

Rev. Dr. Jamie Washington
President, The Washington Consulting Group
President and Cofounder, The Social Justice
Training Institute

Acknowledgments

This book was born from an early idea paper that Scott drafted back in 2014 based on his professional practice as a social justice educator. Special thanks go to Diane Goodman and Jason Garvey for reading and providing feedback on the first iterations of this original idea paper as well as for being supportive of its potential for publication. Additional thanks go to Laila McCloud for being an early thought partner who helped refine the ideas presented in the book and ensured the realities and needs of practitioners were prioritized. Further thanks go to the National Conference on Race and Ethnicity in American Higher Education (NCORE) community who attended the first workshops from which this book was further shaped and encouraged.

Navigating the publishing process for this book required help from a wonderful community of friends and colleagues. Our gratitude goes to David Stovall and Vijay Pendakur for helping think through the earliest stages of the book publishing process. Additional thanks go to Ariel Gonzalez from the DePaul University Center for Writing-based Learning for their help copyediting the manuscript. Additionally, the entire team from Stylus Publishing was wonderfully gracious with their time and patience when addressing multiple questions and requests from first-time book authors. Specifically, the deepest gratitude goes to our editor John von Knorring, for his support, insight, and suggestions to ensure this book will be useful for the widest range of educators possible.

Last, but not least, we are indebted to our families for their endless encouragement and support to finish this book. Without the help of our partners, Krista and Maria, we could not have balanced our responsibilities that allowed us to find time to write and host regular meetings to talk through the book. Finally, our love and gratitude go to our children who inspired us along the way.

Introduction

Getting Clear About What Does (and Should) Guide Social Justice Education Workshops and Structured Conversations

A review of articles in *The Chronicle of Higher Education* and *Inside Higher Ed* reveal how issues of social (in)justice on college campuses have resurged in the national spotlight in recent years. As student activism has gained attention from university leadership, many student activists have articulated varied demands to enhance the campus climate (Espinosa et al., 2016). An analysis of student demands by Chessman and Wayt (2016) revealed a call for more campus diversity programming and training, curriculum revisions, and an increase in the racial diversity of students on campus. Among the ways that institutions attempted to invest in diversity on their campuses is the creation of diversity workshops and trainings (Kolowich, 2015).

These efforts are moving forward amidst growing social unrest in the United States. The rise of White nationalism and the increased visibility of White supremacist groups (Fieldstadt & Dilanian, 2019) have intensified the urgency of social justice work. More than ever, a greater number of institutions are feeling a sense of urgency to provide their students a strong foundation of racial literacy and American racial history in order to produce a well-educated, interculturally competent, and civically engaged populace.

This book is for educators who create and facilitate social justice education experiences, especially shorter workshops and structured conversations lasting 2 hours or less in a single session. This book is for you if you are an educator who (a) works as a professional staff member on a college campus, (b) is in a student role as either a peer educator or graduate student learning the field, or (c) works in a nonprofit organization that develops educational experiences with college-aged youth. Because of the wide range of educational and professional backgrounds of readers this book wishes to serve, it does not make assumptions about readers' knowledge, awareness, or skills regarding curricula development, facilitation, or assessment. The format for this book seeks to be useful in a few different ways. For some, this book can serve as a textbook for graduate students in courses within the fields of education, higher education, or multicultural education to teach the theoretical knowledge and practical skills necessary for social justice education design, facilitation, and assessment. Relatedly, this book can serve as a training workbook to help develop students serving in peer educator positions. For practitioners, this book can serve as a self-guided workbook to support their practice based on their specific needs or help them to document and improve their practice.

The one assumption this book makes is that readers have some familiarity with social justice education. (If not, multiple sources are cited that may be helpful resources to consider.) This book acknowledges social justice educators may work either on large teams with specific staff members charged with planning and facilitating workshops or serve as "offices of one" and are expected to lead workshops as a small part of their broader role supporting diversity initiatives on campus. Additionally, this book emphasises the importance of collaborative efforts with, and getting the support of, faculty whenever possible, including those who are experts in the fields of education, history, political science, sociology, and psychology. *Credibility* is a word often tossed around by those who question the validity of social justice educators. Having strong faculty support helps social justice educators weather the scrutiny that often comes with doing this work.

Context for Writing This Book

It is common for universities to expect staff in student affairs or specific "diversity" units (e.g., multicultural student departments or institutional equity offices) to create and implement these social justice initiatives. What guides these educators in their work? Nagda et al. (2006) emphasize the importance of using scholarship and best practices to design educational experiences that develop student learning related to cultural competence. However, Bonilla et al. (2012) found that educators do not always follow this wisdom. Why might this be the case?

Multiple books explore various aspects critical to social justice education. For example, Pope et al. (2019) discuss what competencies students should develop. Torres et al. (2003) synthesize multiple theories and conceptual frameworks that guide student development. Adams, Bell, Goodman, and Joshi (2016)[1] provide an overview of social justice education that includes pedagogical considerations, facilitation guidance, and course-based curriculum resources. Zúñiga et al. (2007) provide an overview of intergroup dialogue design and facilitation topics. In addition, Suskie (2009) provides steps to develop learning outcomes along with tools to collect and analyze data related to student learning. While these resources provide key steps in the design, facilitation, and assessment process, none of them engage all of these topics in a single text.

Similarly, there are professional associations and conferences that help educators develop and implement social justice education experiences on campus. The American College Personnel Association (ACPA) and the National Association of Student Personnel Administrators (NASPA) coauthored a set of professional competencies that staff ought to have in their roles. One of these competencies, labeled "social justice and inclusion," includes the ability to "design programs and events that are inclusive, promote social consciousness and challenge current institutional, country, global, and sociopolitical systems of oppression" (ACPA/NASPA, 2016, p. 29). Another competency in the area labeled "student learning and development" includes the ability to "design programs based on current research and theories of student learning and development" (ACPA/NASPA, 2016, p. 31). During the 2019 ACPA annual conference in Boston, they hosted 370 sessions over three days. Of these sessions, 206 were associated with the social justice and inclusion area, and 126 were associated with the student learning and development area (ACPA, 2019).

However, only two session titles explicitly talked about designing curricula associated with social justice education efforts. Similarly, the National Conference on Race and Ethnicity in American Higher Education (NCORE) provides a 4-day conference to help institutions "search for effective strategies to enhance access, social development, education, positive communication, and cross-cultural understanding" (NCORE, n.d.). During the 2019 annual conference hosted in Portland, Oregon, NCORE hosted 339 sessions. However, only 33 sessions listed "curriculum" as a keyword, and only five of these sessions talked about processes to design a curriculum in their descriptions (NCORE, 2019). While these conferences provide training and development for staff to do this work, many sessions displayed either an individual curriculum or models to develop a curriculum specific to a single context.

While scholarship and professional development opportunities exist, they do not always help educators learn how to integrate the broader literature that exists to help them design, facilitate, *and* assess social justice education curricula for themselves. This book remedies this gap by reviewing and synthesizing these literature streams in order to help educators develop, facilitate, and assess curricula they design for their local campus communities. Additionally, this book gives particular attention to the cocurricular contexts in which social justice education occurs. Unlike course-based experiences where faculty have more time to cultivate student learning, many cocurricular experiences occur in the format of either a workshop or a structured conversation. Therefore, this book talks explicitly about how to develop and implement curricula in timeframes common to workshops (2 hours or less) and/or in spaces where student attendance may be optional.

Book Overview

This book is divided into two parts. Part One consists of chapters 1 through 7, which explore steps related to curriculum design, specifically curriculum development, facilitation, and assessment. Chapters are sequentially organized to help readers critically prepare for each step of the curriculum design process, drawing on multiple strands of scholarship. Each chapter includes a discussion of each step, an introduction to key ideas and processes to assist in your future approaches, and personal reflections written in the first person from each of us (Scott and Roger) to

---

[1] The editors of both *Teaching for Diversity and Social Justice* (Adams, Bell, & Griffin, 2007) and *Readings for Diversity and Social Justice* (Adams, Blumenfeld, Castaneda, Hackman, Peters, & Zúñiga, 2013) explicitly requested that all names be cited. Citations from these books adhere to their request.

provide insight regarding how the process plays out with real practitioners and our varied social identities. Additionally, each chapter concludes by applying the content discussed to two fictitious examples that run throughout the book, followed by specific reflection questions to help you apply the content to your own work. Handouts are included after each chapter for readers to copy and complete to help guide you in the process. Visit https://styluspub.presswarehouse.com/browse/book/9781642670370/Doing-Social-Justice-Education to access digital versions of the handouts.

Chapters 1 and 2 start with important considerations *prior* to developing a curriculum. These chapters discuss the educational context along with how readers can use theory to make sense of this context when developing a curriculum. Chapter 1 describes the contextual influences practitioners should identify and address throughout the educational experience. This chapter focuses on seven contextual influences related to the students, the environment, and the educators themselves. Chapter 2 explores multiple theoretical and conceptual frameworks practitioners can use when developing a curriculum. This chapter pays specific attention to the assumptions of each framework and how educators might apply these frameworks to various contextual influences discussed in the first chapter. The goal of both chapters is to help readers critically discern which frameworks are helpful when addressing various contextual influences for the goal of meeting students where they are in their development.

Chapters 3 and 4 pivot to considerations *during* curriculum design related to actual outcomes and activities. These chapters build on the previously discussed contextual influences and frameworks to inform the actual curriculum. Chapter 3 provides a process to identify learning areas for the experience and then develop them into specific learning outcome statements. Additionally, this chapter explains how to distill ambitious goals for educators' work into realistic expectations for student learning given the boundaries of the educational experience. Chapter 4 describes pedagogical considerations practitioners should follow to ensure a curriculum is congruent with the essence of social justice education. Common activity types, including guidelines, task-based activities, and discussion-based activities, are discussed in a modular fashion to construct a curriculum that adheres to these pedagogical considerations.

Chapters 5 and 6 turn to considerations after the curriculum is developed and implemented. These chapters explore how to facilitate and assess a curriculum. Chapter 5 examines technical aspects of facilitation along with preparation strategies educators might consider prior to facilitation. Chapter 6 explores the process of assessing student learning through established learning outcome statements. This chapter shares a simplified, five-step process for assessment along with three common tools for collecting and analyzing data. An overview of each tool precedes tips for developing these tools along with examples of ways to use each tool to collect data during or after the educational experience.

While chapters 1 through 6 refer explicitly to in-person experiences, chapter 7 reflects on how educators support online learning experiences. This chapter explores additional considerations for educators related to both fully online and blended experiences depending on the technology, software platform, and format used for teaching. An overview of each step discussed in chapters 1 through 6 is reexamined to highlight how they remain useful for online teaching and learning.

Part Two consists of chapters 8 through 10, which provide examples of real workshops and structured conversations that were developed, facilitated, and assessed (or how they could have been assesed). Examples come from educational experiences in different settings. Chapter 8 describes a workshop embedded in a required class for all first-year students. Chapter 9 explores a structured conversation to promote racial dialogue and literacy among students on campus. Chapter 10 discusses a workshop implemented with a national nonprofit organization for student scholarship recipients going into education. These different examples highlight the versatility of this approach to support a wide array of student contexts and institutional backgrounds.

Personal Reflection and Positionality

The concept of *praxis*, or reflection on action that guides further action, is a central component of social justice education. Freire (2000) stated that reflection is essential for action. Reflection that does not lead to action may be little more than navel gazing. Action without reflection does not have a path for improvement and growth. However, when reflection and action are purposefully connected, they provide critical insights into oneself and one's work.

This book promotes praxis in two ways. First, a list of questions exists at the end of each chapter for readers to reflect purposefully on their practice to determine their own path when designing, facilitating, and assessing social justice education experiences. The contents of this book guide educators through a process of creating and implementing curricula themselves. Therefore, readers should pause at the end of each chapter and use the reflection questions to guide their own action.

Second, first-person reflections from the authors about the content is interwoven in most chapters. As chapter 1 describes, social identities influence the way we, as social justice educators, engage this work. Readers may understand this material in different ways that yield different approaches to the work. Positionality matters because it influences our approach to social justice education (Bell, Goodman, & Varghese, 2016). How we think about our own social identities through the lens of our experiences of privilege and oppression matter. Therefore, the authors' reflections illustrate how we make sense of the content discussed in this book. One approach is neither better nor worse than another. Instead, our approaches reflect how we understand the world and how we bring that understanding to bear on our choices when we develop and implement workshops and structured conversations. We cannot expect readers to reflect on their practice if we do not model this for ourselves. Therefore, we would like to introduce ourselves so that readers know the voices and perspectives embedded in the book.

Scott
I identify with several privileged social identities. I am a White, cisgender, male, able-bodied, U.S. citizen, English-speaker who was raised Catholic and is currently middle class. However, I also identify with two oppressed social identities, including being born into a working-class family and identifying as a non-Christian who follows earth-based spirituality. These intersecting social identities created a distinctive experience that fueled my passion for social justice education.

I grew up in a White working-class family where I was socialized into Whiteness with a strong belief in rugged individualism. My family seldom discussed our own White experiences and instead focused on the importance of hard work and financial security. When family or friends brought up race, it was framed predominantly

in ways that positioned "us" as hardworking and deserving relative to "them" who were lazy and undeserving. These beliefs were cemented through my experiences in middle school and high school where gangs were mostly Black and Latinx, and students in advanced courses were mostly White. As a result, my understanding of privilege and oppression mirrored that of many other working-class Whites who have a meritocratic view of the world that masks racial inequities.

I did not begin exploring my privileged social identities, including my Whiteness, until college. Two pivotal moments occurred in my life. First, I navigated discrimination against me as a non-Christian, which cultivated empathy for other oppressed groups. It was through conversations with others about these experiences that challenged me to consider how I contribute to discrimination from my privileged social identities. Second, I completed a course on eugenics and the Holocaust that illustrated how beliefs in superiority were structurally infused in institutional practices and policies that persist today. These two experiences collectively helped me use my oppressed identities as approximating experiences (Feagin et al., 2001) to examine my personal contributions to systemic inequality related to race, gender, sexuality, and ability status. My awakening to systemic privilege inspired my decision to pursue graduate education in social work and curriculum studies to develop educational interventions in higher education to educate students, specifically students with privileged social identities, to develop the capacity to dismantle systemic privilege.

My career in higher education spans 12 years in roles that either oversaw the design, facilitation, and assessment of social justice education initiatives for students, faculty, and staff on campus or oversaw assessment and evaluation practices for student affairs. I continue this work as a staff member, adjunct faculty member, scholar, and consultant. I evolved past my original socialization; however, those memories and experiences continue to provide rich insight into students from privileged groups who struggle to acknowledge privilege. As a result, my approach to social justice education entails empathy with accountability. I always want to acknowledge the real feelings students from privileged groups have while coupling that with accountability so that these feelings do not result in privilege paralysis *that halts action for social change. Additionally, I conscientiously work to ensure my social identities and beliefs do not center social justice education solely on privileged groups. Therefore, I constantly reflect* on my approach to consider how it will impact students from multiple oppressed social identities.

Roger

My mother, Iris Milagros Gonzales Rios, was born and raised in Jayuya, Puerto Rico. She and her siblings grew up poor. My grandmother did whatever jobs were necessary to make ends meet while my grandfather moved to Chicago to work as a chef at a northside hospital. At 17, my mom, along with my grandmother and my two aunts, joined my grandfather on the Windy City's north side.

My father, Nelson Alfredo Moreano, was a train engineer and worked at various manufacturing jobs in Quito, Ecuador, where he was born and raised. After several of his siblings had relocated to the United States, my dad, the last of 19 kids and at age 28, left for Patterson, New Jersey, where one brother had been living. After a few years living in Patterson and working in New York City, he relocated to Chicago where he met my mother and where I was born.

I come to social justice from my life experience. Growing up with Spanish as my first language, I remember struggling to learn English in schools. I grew up with my dual heritages coexisting beautifully—on one side, my Puerto Rican family, a loud and proud familia who were a diverse mix of Brown, Black and White uncles, aunts, cousins, and close friends we also considered primos and primas and tíos and tías. I have vivid memories of the aroma of my abuelita's arroz con gandules, the overpowering smell of my grandfather's nightly cigar, and the savory tostones that would sizzle in the kitchen of that second-floor apartment on Clark Street. Holidays meant listening to Celia Cruz, Willie Colón, and Eddie Palmieri playing loudly through the living room speakers and begging my mom to stay up later to dance with the grown-ups.

My Ecuadorian heritage was just as present as we spent time eating ceviche, eating Fanesca at Easter time, playing the card game "Cuarenta" with my cousins, aunts, and uncles, and listening to endless rotations of the music of Julio Jaramillo. We were a lower-middle class Catholic family who twice had to move in and live with my cousins' families during my youth. At age 7, we moved to the Gulf coast of Florida, as my father had been unemployed for months and was desperate to find work. After 8 months in Florida, and with my father still unemployed, we returned to Chicago. My father, who was the only parent employed in my younger years, spent time moving from factory job to factory job as lay-offs occurred with regularity. His misfortune also greatly affected me personally, as I found myself attending six different schools by the time I reached the fourth grade. Finally, at age 9, my father found work in the northern suburbs of Chicago where I attended high school and college.

As I grew up, I saw how other people often mocked my mother and father for their strong accents when they spoke. I found myself regularly code-switching between worlds as I engaged in Little League baseball, long country bike rides, and walks to the beach in an all-White suburb, then reacclimating to city life and the norms of my family when we visited them in Chicago on the weekends. These experiences forged a strong impression on me as I grappled with ideas of "belonging" and "fitting in" and how these shaped my worldview. As time went on, I connected over and over again with those in society who did not "fit in." By my mid-20s I was led to this work.

With an undergraduate degree in political science and international relations, a minor in history, and a master's degree in business administration, my career imperative became to live my passion through my profession. I have worked in higher education since 1997 and have led equity and inclusion work since 2002. In 2016, I launched a consulting business to bring social justice education and training to K–12 school districts.

I believe that we cannot separate our work from who we are at our core. At my core, I am a person who has had a life full of experiences of being "othered." I have known what it is like to feel that I, and my identities, do not belong. I immediately recognize when marginalization happens to friends, neighbors, family, coworkers, and students. My deep hunger for a more equitable world has led me to a career path that reflects who I am and to work to develop programs, workshops, and experiences designed to have folks wrestle deeply with important questions of identity, belonging, and authenticity. In these programs, I consistently work to build community in our shared space, to have our authentic stories shared, to help the voiceless find their voice, to have participants see the intersectionality of oppressive systems, and to ultimately lay a foundation for potential transformative breakthroughs to occur.

As a human being who believes in the inherent worth and dignity of all fellow human beings, I remain committed to working to dismantle the social, political, economic, and educational barriers that for millennia have kept countless individuals and entire communities from expressing the fullness of their humanity and potential. I *hope this text lays a foundation for readers as they confidently tackle the work that is necessary to carry humanity and, more immediately, our campuses forward.*

Authors' Stance

Paulo Freire's educational approach is one anchor of social justice education. Among his many contributions to this work, he explicitly states in *Pedagogy of the Oppressed* (Freire, 2000) that all education is political and should serve a larger project for social justice. Therefore, it is necessary to articulate the political stance this book has as it contributes to the larger project of social justice. This book's primary purpose is to support educators in their practice to ensure congruence between the content and processes related to our work. In doing so, we adopt the following stances toward this goal. First, we share Bell's (2007) definition that *social justice* is both a process and a goal. Therefore, this book provides content to help readers think through the goals of their work and a process for doing it well. We describe a student-centered, inclusive process for educators to use before, during, and after curricula are developed. Additionally, we provide personal reflections to highlight and model the necessity of personal reflection to ensure our intrapersonal approach to this work is congruent with social justice education processes.

Second, we acknowledge that social justice education is a broad topic that encapsulates multiple sociocultural categories and social identities. We are selective when discussing social identities to enhance readability, primarily exploring race, gender, sexuality, religion, social class, and ability status. Every attempt was made to discuss the content of this book through each of these lenses. However, it does not reflect the belief that other sociocultural categories, social identities, and systems of privilege and oppression do not matter. At the same time, we acknowledge that we situated this book within the context of the United States, which has a distinctive history of racial privilege and oppression that has provided a foundation (and perhaps the roadmap) for how other systems of dominance were developed and integrated in society. Therefore, we intentionally lean into racial examples to acknowledge this sociological truth and provide explicit support for the great project of racial justice through educational interventions.

Third, we believe that educators should be empowered to develop, facilitate, and assess curricula

that they ground in the localized reality and experience of their students. While there is a movement that is working to standardize education, we do not share this vision. Instead, we believe that educators should tailor educational experiences to the needs of the community and never standardize these experiences at the expense of flexibility to meet the needs of students. That said, we do believe that education should be an intentional process guided by our knowledge of our students, relevant theoretical and conceptual frameworks, established learning outcomes, and purposefully curated activities. For these reasons, this book provides an intentional process to guide educators in their work at the local level. It provides multiple examples embedded in content chapters and as standalone chapters to illuminate how this process works in order to help educators critically discern how to move forward for themselves. However, these examples are not provided as "canned workshops," and we hope that readers do not use them in this way.

Fourth, we acknowledge there are multiple paths to intentionally develop, facilitate, and assess curricula. This book provides one way to approach this process. However, we hope readers do not misinterpret our process as superior to other processes. The intent behind this book is to provide educators a way to guide their work. If you find that there are other considerations you want to address, other theories you find useful, or a different sequence for the process, please use them! We offer this model as a starting point to help in your work, so do what helps you provide the best educational experience for your students to support their learning. As such, we hope this book serves as a metaphorical diving board that launches you into the water.

Key Terms and Concepts

This book uses language that is consistent with the streams of scholarship used. However, since some terms and their use may be less familiar to all readers, we want to be clear about commonly used terms, how we define them, and why we have made these choices.

Social Justice

Lee Ann Bell (2007) defines *social justice* as "both a process and a goal" (p. 6) that uses democratic, pluralistic, and critically conscious processes to facilitate the development of knowledge, attitudes, and skills for social change that lead to the "full and equal participation of all groups . . . shaped to meet their needs" (pp. 1–2). Social justice is a concept that examines topics beyond social and cultural differences, that terms such as *diversity* and *multiculturalism* often also examine. We adopt the language of social justice to highlight the importance of structural and institutional forces that shape the manifestation of social power afforded to social groups.

Privilege and Oppression

Educators can describe the inequitable manifestation of social power using various terms such as *dominant/ subordinate*, *marginalization*, and *minoritization*. While these terms are useful, we adopt the language of privilege and oppression commonly used in social justice education that explicitly connects this work to the broader social justice education literature. We define *privilege* as the rights, benefits, and access to resources granted (i.e., privilege) or denied (i.e., oppression) to people based on their social identities at an individual and an institutional level via social power. This definition is guided by the broader scholarship on privilege (Hardiman, Jackson, & Griffin, 2007; Johnson, 2006; McIntosh, 1989; Winant, 1997) and oppression (Adams, Blumenfeld, Castañeda, Hackman, Peters, & Zúñiga, 2013; Fanon, 1963, 1967; Freire, 2000; Hardiman, Jackson, & Griffin, 2007). Furthermore, this definition reinforces the dialectical relationship between these two terms, highlighting how *privilege* and *oppression* necessarily coexist because of the presence of one another. Using these terms allows us to describe both the lived experiences of individuals that are manufactured through these structural forces and the structural forces themselves. As a result, we use these terms together frequently in the book to make these connections explicit.

Social Identity

Tajfel and Turner (1979) first coined the term *social identity* to describe a social group to which a collection of individuals identifies a sense of belonging. This definition aptly highlights the social and individual nature of social identity. Additionally, this definition is more encompassing than the term *cultural identity*, which connotes a connection to a specific cultural way of life.

Curricula

This book discusses repeatedly the creation of curricula. *Curricula* are often used to describe a formalized collection of courses or lessons, such as a liberal studies curriculum. However, we use this term in its broadest sense to refer to educational expectations and structured associated activities used to promote student learning. In this sense of the term, *curricula* live beyond traditional courses when intentionally developed. Therefore, curricular spaces (e.g., courses) and cocurricular spaces (e.g., programs and workshops outside of courses) may claim to both develop and use curricula. For this book, we use this term to highlight the intentional development of social justice education experiences and to demonstrate how this work manifests itself in cocurricular spaces.

Conclusion

As the late Senator Paul Wellstone was known for saying, "We all do better when we all do better." We hope this book provides you with the knowledge and tools necessary to guide your work to advance social justice education within your local community of students. May this resource help us do our work better so that both educators and students collectively can do better for social justice.

A PROCESS TO DESIGN, FACILITATE, AND ASSESS SOCIAL JUSTICE EDUCATION WORKSHOPS AND STRUCTURED CONVERSATIONS

CHAPTER 1

Contextual Influences

"Educators need to know what happens in the world of the children with whom they work."
—Paulo Freire (1998, p. 72)

It is important that educators design curricula for workshops and structured conversations with respect to what students already know and need. While this statement may seem obvious, it bears repeating as a necessary first step when developing a curriculum. Students are not an empty bucket waiting for educators to fill their heads with information. Instead, learners come to every education experience with prior knowledge (Ambrose et al., 2010) that influences how they participate and what they are likely to gain from the experience.

These views are consistent with a sociocultural approach to education, or a view that education is socially influenced. Lev Vygotsky (1978) championed a sociocultural view and explained that the interactions one has with others, and their social environment, is particularly influential on student learning. This idea was expanded on by Lave and Wenger's (1991) scholarship on situated learning theory. Situated learning theory asserts that learning is an inherently social practice grounded in social and cultural reproduction (Lave & Wenger, 1991). As such, learning occurs all the time, including in informal settings. What people watch on television, read online, witness walking down the street, and experience in relationships provides information used to shape and reshape their understanding of themselves, others, and society.

Issues that are central to social justice education, such as diversity, privilege, and oppression, are always present in a social environment. Because this is a world

where social differences are constantly around, one cannot insulate themselves from these issues. Sometimes these issues are explicit, such as during conversations about race. Other times, they are implicit, such as during interactions with people who are racially different or conversations that involve race without naming race. For example, an explicit conversation about immigration border security in the United States most often implies a racial problem with Latinxs (specifically Mexicans) but not White people (specifically White Canadians). Therefore, any time someone participates in a conversation about immigration border security, they are simultaneously engaging a racialized way of thinking about the world. In these moments, individuals are gathering information about race that they carry with them into any learning environment. Therefore, students use their prior knowledge about race regardless of whether or not they have had a formal educational experience where they learned about race. Because social justice content centers on issues of social identity and power, most students have some level of prior knowledge about social justice education issues, regardless of how accurate that knowledge may be.

Students may have a variety of needs that derive from the prior knowledge they bring to social justice workshops and structured conversations. These different needs may become more distinctive depending on their year in school. First-year students may be trying to discern the racial climate on campus and engage conversations with hesitance. Students about to graduate may already have established ways of engaging racial topics depending on who is in the room. Students' needs may vary based on both their prior knowledge and their immediate environment.

11

Because a student's social environment influences what they need and how they might participate in a learning experience, educators should consider relevant contextual factors that may influence the learning experience. Multiple scholars assert the importance of developing an educational experience with respect to the student's experience and environment. L. Dee Fink's (2013) scholarship on backward educational design emphasized how educators must take into account the context of the learning environment and student characteristics when designing an educational experience. Bell and Griffin's (2007) insights about developing social justice education courses emphasized the necessity of aligning the unique social identities and related experiences of students to develop appropriate learning goals and design an impactful learning environment for social justice. Paulo Freire's (2000) pedagogy for dialogical education also emphasized the importance of a student-centered approach that intentionally builds on the existing knowledge and experiences of students. Collectively, these contextual considerations of students in their environment are essential. Understanding students' lives, knowledge, and interests within their educational, campus, and social contexts can be useful in the design of student-centered workshops.

When developing a social justice education curriculum for workshops and structured conversations, there are seven contextual factors that educators should consider (see Figure 1.1). These factors involve the educators themselves, the students, and the students' environment.

Yourself, the Educator

When considering contextual influences on student learning, it is often forgotten that you, the educator, are an influence on students worthy of consideration. You not only shape the design and facilitation of the social justice workshop or structured conversation but also are another person in the local educational environment to which students will react during the educational experience. Therefore, it is vital for educators to take time to reflect on who they are, how their prior knowledge shapes the way they create educational experiences for students, and how their active and passive presence influences students during the facilitation of a workshop or structured conversation.

FIGURE 1.1. Contextual influences on social justice education.

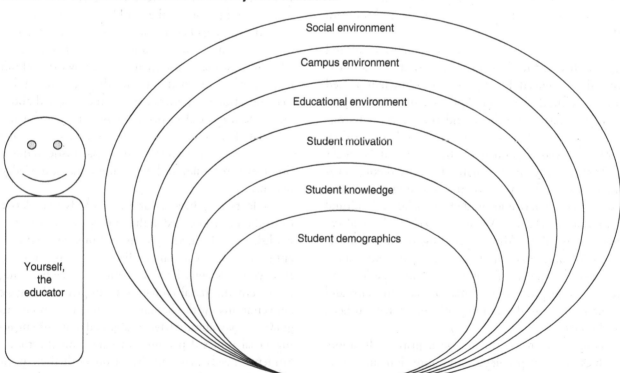

It is essential to identify that the social identities you hold are central to both how you understand social justice education and how students will react to you as part of the educational environment. At the most basic level, it is important to acknowledge your various social identities and how those social identities experience privilege or oppression within society. The intersectional model of multiple dimensions of identity (I-MMDI) developed by Jones, Abes and Quaye (as cited in Jones & Abes, 2013) provides a useful framework to consider how individuals make meaning of the multitude of social identities present in their lives within the broader social environment in which they live. This model explains how lived experiences with multiple and intersecting social identities exist within a broader social context of power (see chapter 2 for a fuller discussion). For example, individuals make sense of their sexual orientation through both their individual sexual identity and the broader social context of heterosexism that shapes their day-to-day lives. Further, this model underscores how the various social identities intersect in ways that also shape our understanding of social identities. A few examples may help clarify this point.

I (Scott) identify as a White person who grew up in a working-class social class (I write "grew up" because, as an adult, I have become middle class). I experience White privilege in numerous ways, such as being viewed as credible when I challenge a price check at the grocery store, being comfortable in most social spaces that include mostly White people and are centered around White norms, and having the opportunity to find professional mentors who look like me. Additionally, I grew up experiencing oppression as a working-class youth in numerous ways, such as being ridiculed by my peers for not affording name-brand groceries and clothing, not having knowledge of professional attire standards (I was once rated poorly at a speech tournament for not knowing to leave the bottom button of my suit jacket unbuttoned), and not having family members to help me navigate a college search process. However, I grew up viewing myself as a member of a "White, working-class" oppressed group. Even though I was White and experienced White privilege, I could not readily see my racial experience and advantages through the lens of my working-class oppression. Further, I grew up in a family where there was an adamant belief that Latinxs were taking away working-class jobs from Whites, and this anchored how I saw myself as oppressed as a White, working-class person. Therefore, the ways I made

sense of my White social identity and working-class social identity were intertwined for the bulk of my youth until halfway through my undergraduate studies. The result of my sense-making was that I was quick to reject conversations about White privilege and instead found issues of social class oppression to be more relevant. Even though I have evolved in my understanding of my White privilege, I am still shaped by these social identities that have inspired a life-long passion for an intersectional analysis of race and social class. Therefore, whenever I create or facilitate social justice education workshops or structured conversations, I am more likely to see and engage themes of race and social class because of my social identities and associated journey.

I (Roger) am keenly aware of how my Latinx social identity does and does not show up in my facilitation. As "the lighter one" in my family, my White-passing identity has allowed me access to spaces that would no doubt be more challenging or off limits to fellow colleagues of color. Having also grown up since age 9 in a White suburban environment, I developed a good sense of Whiteness norms and how they showed up in social spaces. Indeed, my White passing appearance (is he Italian? Is he Jewish? Is he Greek? Is he . . . ?) often led to what I would deem an unspoken acceptance of my place in the White social circles where I found myself located. With that acceptance came the unconscious comfort others felt in showing their true colors. Racial jokes making fun of Brown and Black folk and disrespecting non-Christian faith traditions were experiences I dealt with on occasion.

As a professional who has worked exclusively at predominantly White institutions (PWIs), I have students of color who, each year, share similar experiences with me. I work intentionally to build space in my programs and workshops to empower students of color to speak their truth while being vulnerable in sharing their fears. From code-switching to standing up for oneself against inequity and injustice, the programs I develop need to be rich with messages of encouragement, empowerment, and pride in one's social identity. The messages empower students to be more authentic and to consider their social identities just as "valid" and important as the dominant identities on campus and in society. As one student named Ivan related to me, "For years I made sure I pronounced my name "Eye-Van" because it sounded more acceptable to the mainstream." After returning from a series of on- and off-campus programs, Ivan made it known he was reclaiming his sense of self and that his name was pronounced "EE-Von."

In addition to the ways in which social identities shape educators' approach to social justice education, educators also bring them into the educational environment that they facilitate. Therefore, educators also need to consider how their social identities show up, for both themselves as well as the students in the learning environment. The extent to which educators acknowledge their multiple, intersecting social identities; are conscious of how they perform those identities; and are aware of how students perceive and react to their identities will influence the environment.

For example, I (Roger), as a Latinx man, consistently reference my cultural norms (e.g., speaking Spanish) and infuse those norms into my vernacular and demeanor with regularity. I do this for a couple of reasons. First, I want to role model for students and colleagues what it looks like to live authentically by embracing my roots. I want to inculcate the idea that as a man of color I can navigate the systems I operate in by not giving up who I am or acting out in ways that communicate submission to the dominant culture. I see this approach as having a positive impact in workshops I facilitate as I consistently receive feedback from students of color feeling like they had "permission" to be themselves. Second, I am well aware that how I show up in these spaces is also affecting majority students. I make sure to go out of my way to communicate and offer space for folks with privilege to be able to express themselves in ways that can be authentic. However, I want them to see me as an example of someone who is comfortable in my identity and as the facilitator and navigator of the dialogical experience. In doing so, I go out of my way to assure all students that there will likely be two things happening simultaneously in the dialogue. First, students will be engaging in a space that will give them permission to be authentic. Second, students will be challenged to see systems and behaviors that are discriminatory and often unconscious (e.g., Whiteness, maleness) and further challenged to recognize how these systems impact the whole. Without being mindful and intentional in how I show up into these spaces, I would be unable to set the stage for productive and impactful connections to take place.

I (Scott), as a White man doing social justice education, need to think critically about my Whiteness and maleness prior to every workshop in order to ensure that I am not replicating Whiteness and maleness in the educational spaces that I facilitate. Further, I need to actively scan the room for student reactions to see if I am performing my social identities in a way that may contradict the *message of the workshop or structured conversation. In my experience facilitating workshops in predominantly White spaces, I find that White students seem more willing to participate because I am White. However, I also notice cautious engagement among students of color who may have reasonable doubts about how I approach social justice education topics given their past experiences with White staff and faculty on campus. Overall, it is imperative that I am aware of these dynamics and constantly reflecting on them as part of my job as a facilitator.*

Student Factors

It is useful to think about the students who will participate in the educational experience. When considering the students, it is helpful to reflect on who they are, what knowledge and experience they already have, and what motivates their decision to participate in the workshop or structured conversation. Each of these reflections corresponds with examining students' demographics, knowledge, and motivation, respectively.

It is important to know some demographic characteristics about these students. Having a demographic profile provides insight into any commonalities and differences among these students that may influence how they engage the educational experience. A demographic profile of students should at least include their social identities, class standing, and academic majors or roles. Roles refer to the type of leadership or employment position they may have on campus such as resident advisers or orientation leaders. Knowing the academic majors or roles of students are useful because, like social identities and class standing, they provide information that can help educators frame content and questions around common needs (e.g., checking assumptions of resident advisers when enforcing policies) and interests (e.g., exploring human diversity to help theater majors understand characters). Information about the overall student body's social identities, class standing, and majors are likely available through the campus institutional research or admissions office. Educators can obtain information about students in specific roles by asking the supervisor for these positions.

Related to who the students are is what prior knowledge they bring with them. Students' prior knowledge might include knowledge derived from previous formal educational experiences (e.g., common coursework or training) or informal experiences (e.g., interactive or immersive experiences) shared among the learners who attended a workshop. It will also be useful to consider whether or not the students have already reached conclusions about relevant topics from these experiences. For example, students may have previously had an immersion experience in a racially segregated community, completed a diversity activity where they reflected on their personal privilege, or experienced a tense debate about affirmative action that ended early due to time. The easiest way to receive this information is to explore likely common experiences shared among these students (e.g., a standardized orientation experience or required first-year seminar course) and identify any intended or unintended takeaways from these experiences. If a specific person or department requested a workshop or structured conversation, the facilitator can also ask them to share what they know about these students.

Lastly, what motivates students to participate in the educational experience is equally important. In some cases, students may be required to attend a workshop or structured conversation as part of job training or an academic course. In other cases, students could receive an incentive to participate in the form of extra credit. Other students may be strongly motivated by a desire for personal or professional development. Each of these motivation forces may shape the way students show up and participate in the experience. One of the worst assumptions that can be made is that all students are demographically the same, have the same needs, and think about social justice education content the same way. Such assumptions are both untrue and contradict the essence of social justice education that affirms the importance of pluralism.

Environmental Factors

The environment in which students exist is equally as important to know as the students themselves. First, it is helpful to consider the educational environment where the workshop or structured conversation will occur. Knowing if the environment is curricular (a workshop offered during a class) or cocurricular (a workshop offered during job training) can yield insights into the student factors discussed previously as well as yield additional insight into the group

dynamics among the students. Curricular environments are often influenced by variables beyond the control of the students, such as class availability, when courses are offered, and if the course is a major requirement or an elective. However, students often opt into cocurricular environments due to a common interest. Related to the curricular or cocurricular environment is how frequently these students come together as a group. There is a difference when creating an experience for students who meet regularly versus those who do not. The logistics about the workshop within this context is relevant, such as how long the workshop will last and when it will occur relative to the life span of the group.

All educational environments exist within a broader campus environment. What happens on campus can and will influence both the students and the educational environment where workshops and structured conversations will occur. Multiple campus environment factors can be relevant. These most often include lingering perceptions and specific incidents.

Lingering perceptions refer to beliefs held by students toward the campus, staff, faculty, and other students associated with policies or behaviors. Perceptions can be either positive or negative and can be shared openly with others or kept to themselves. For example, students with minoritized social identities may have private negative perceptions of the campus and the administration because of pervasive treatment they have received and that they discuss with one another among themselves on campus. Meanwhile, White students may have positive public perceptions of the campus because they view it as "sufficiently diverse." Relatedly, specific incidents refer to campus occurrences that create new or highlight existing campus climate concerns. For example, if an institution invites a speaker to campus who advocates for the oppression of various marginalized groups, that can create tensions on campus. Both lingering perceptions and specific incidents affect the extent to which students feel physically or psychologically safe when participating in a social justice workshop or structured conversation. If students do not feel safe on campus, they are more likely to be withdrawn or defensive during the educational experience. These behaviors may also influence how other students participate in the experience, creating a challenging environment for the educator. Overall, if lingering perceptions exist, or if the campus is recovering after a specific incident, it is likely to manifest itself within the educational environment. When considering lingering perceptions, it is important to consider what the educator knows and does not know, sees and does not see, and hears and does not hear because of their own positionality. A great resource to get a pulse on campus rumblings is to consult the student newspaper or to ask students who are "in the know" about student feelings on campus.

Lastly, the campus environment is situated within a broader social environment that is equally influential. The social environment includes the local community, state, and country where the campus is located. Most often, this will include the news and events discussed in the mainstream and campus social and print media. For example, if an educator is preparing a workshop or structured conversation about gender and gender inequality, they might consider the impact of the #MeToo movement nationally and any incidents of sexual assault on or near campus that students may be thinking about during the educational experience. However, media sources that cover topics relevant to specific social identity groups may also be important to follow to know what is on the minds of specific groups of students. For example, there has been increased attention in the mainstream media about police killings of Black men with the murders of Eric Garner, Michael Brown, Laquan McDonald, Tamir Rice and others (Hafner, 2018). However, the long history of police brutality against racial minorities (Nodjimbadem, 2017) is not new to many Black individuals who have witnessed these concerns or learned about them from other media outlets (NewsOne Staff, 2015), including being discussed widely on social media. Often, mainstream news media does not cover the news and events that may circulate among students within minoritized communities that reflect their interests and needs.

When considering current news and events, it is critical to understand that students may consume news differently from educators. According to a study about journalism habits and perceptions, younger Americans are less likely to trust traditional media outlets and are increasingly likely to use social media as a source of information (Media Insight Project, 2018). Further, the vast majority of young adults use social media platforms including YouTube, Facebook, Instagram, and Snapchat (Perrin & Anderson, 2019), where news and events are often circulated by individuals, companies,

and established news outlets alike. Therefore, it may be useful to broaden both news sources and platforms, to be aware of topics trending on social media, or to keep an ear to the ground to listen for what broader social issues students are carrying with them on campus and into their educational environments.

The following is a detailed list of questions regarding each of the seven influences. These questions may be useful when considering various contextual influences:

Personal awareness

- What social identities (e.g., race, ethnicity, gender, gender expression, sexuality, social class, ability status, religion, age) do you have that are most salient to this workshop or structured conversation?
- How do you enact those social identities during the workshop or structured conversation?
- How might your salient identities impact the facilitation of the workshop or structured conversation?

Student demographics

- What social identities (e.g., race, ethnicity, gender, gender expression, sexuality, social class, ability status, religion, age) are present among students who will participate in the workshop or structured conversation?

  o Which social identities are most salient for the students in the group?

  o Which social identity groups are present yet underrepresented among these students?

- What role(s) (e.g., students at large, student employees) do the students have in common with one another?
- What other identities or characteristics (e.g., geographical region of origin, first-generation college students, undocumented students) are relevant to the group or the content of the workshop or structured conversation?
- Are there any common characteristics shared by these students that may be useful when developing the workshop or structured conversation?

Student knowledge

- What relevant, formal educational experiences (e.g., courses) have these students completed prior to this workshop or structured conversation?
- What relevant, informal educational experiences (e.g., immersion trips) have these students completed prior to this workshop or structured conversation?
- How might these experiences shape their understanding of the content to be covered in the workshop or structured conversation?
- What do you know about how these students tend to think about the topic of the workshop or structured conversation?
- How useful might it be to plan your workshop or structured conversation to engage/build on any of their prior knowledge?

Student motivation

- Why are students attending this workshop or structured conversation?
- What might entice students to be active participants during the workshop or structured conversation?

Educational environment

- What content related to the workshop or structured conversation has already been covered in this setting? When, and in what way?
- How much time has been allocated for the workshop or structured conversation?
- Are there any group dynamics that could influence the workshop or structured conversation experience?
- Is there a need for prep work before you begin to address previous experiences with workshops or structured conversations on this topic?

Campus environment

- Are there any recent campus events that will influence how students think about, or approach, the content of the workshop or structured conversation?

- Generally, do students feel safe to engage in diversity and social justice topics on campus? Does this level of safety look different based on students' salient social identities?
- What messages does the campus communicate about topics related to diversity and social justice?
- To what extent would it be useful to incorporate campus issues to increase the workshop or structured conversation's relevance from the point of view of these students?

Social environment

- What relevant local-level (e.g., neighborhood, town) issues may influence how students show up, or think about, the workshop or structured conversation content?
- What relevant state-level issues may influence how students show up, or think about, the workshop or structured conversation content?
- What relevant national-level issues may influence how students show up, or think about, the workshop or structured conversation content?
- To what extent might different students view these relevant issues differently? How might that influence the workshop or structured conversation?
- To what extent would it be useful to incorporate social issues to increase students' perception of the workshop or structured conversation as relevant?

Information about yourself as the educator, the students, and their environment is necessary to collect and consider when developing social justice education workshops and structured conversations. Knowledge about these contextual influences can ensure that the curriculum you design is relevant to students, appropriate for the environment, and conscientious of how you as the educator influence, and are perceived by, the students in the educational environment. Educators can collect this information prior to designing the educational experience by asking questions about the students, staying informed about current events, and reflecting on your positionality. At the very least, educators should consider doing the following:

- Follow campus news and events using both campus newspapers and social media.
- Stay up to date on local, national, and international news and events.
- Be aware of trending social media topics relevant to the student community or the topics you may be discussing.
- Find out about the local context in which the educational experience will occur.
- Identify any shared educational experiences students may have already completed.
- Seek information from the institutional research department about the student body, including demographic characteristics and campus climate survey data. If demographic characteristics are not available, consider conducting a survey of the students who will attend prior to the experience.
- Regularly reflect on your social identities and how you perform those social identities.

To illustrate how educators can use this framework to develop, facilitate, and assess social justice education workshops and structured conversations, let us apply our discussions to two fictitious institutions. Western College is developing an introductory social justice workshop for residential students. Southeastern University is developing a structured dialogue to address campus concerns.

Western College

Western College (WC) is a small, private college located in the western part of the United States. WC is a designated Hispanic-serving institution (HSI) where its 2,000 students are 35% Latin/a/o/x, 30% White, 15% multiracial, 13% Asian American, 5% percent Black, and 2% international. Nearly 80% of WC's students are Pell Grant eligible and about 21% are first-generation college students. WC does not collect information about students' religious identity or sexual orientation; however, they do collect information about students' gender identity where 50% of students identify at women, 45% of students identify as men, and 5% of students identify as gender nonconforming.

WC resides in a small suburb outside of a small town of 60,000 people that mirrors the racial and economic demographics of the student body. The town's population is fairly liberal and very welcoming of the college and their students. The college and the town have a good relationship, and many campus programs take place off-campus, including at the local feminist bookstore.

On campus, the housing office recently decided to provide all-gender housing to all students to increase inclusivity and respect the gender identity of students. Overall, the campus community has been supportive of this approach; however, some first-year students struggle to understand the purpose and benefits of all-gender housing. To enhance students' understanding of gender, resident advisers regularly provide programs to breakdown stereotypes and misconceptions about sex, gender identity, and gender expression. Specifically, the Office of Residence Life expects all resident advisers to provide a short workshop on sex and gender within the first month of the academic year that explores these concepts and encourages thoughtful peer interactions in the halls. Given this context, gender is a topic of great interest and an extremely salient social identity among students, ultimately benefiting the resident advisers when creating workshops and recruiting students to attend these experiences.

Southeastern University

Southeastern University (SU) is a large, public university located in the southeastern part of the United States. While SU, a historically White institution, has increased their recruitment of students of color, they still have more White, non-Latinx students than any other racial group. The racial make-up of the 30,000 students on campus is 40% White, 35% Black, 10% Asian, 10% Latinx, and 5% international students. Nearly half of SU's students are Pell Grant eligible and about one third are first-generation college students. SU does not collect information about students' religion or sexual orientations but does collect information about students' sex in binary terms only. As a result, 60% of students identify as female while 40% identify as male.

SU resides in the downtown area of a large city that looks different racially from the campus. The city itself is home to 3 million people, 60% of whom are Black, 30% of whom are White, and the remaining 10% are either Asian American or Latin/a/o/x. The city's population is highly racially segregated and hosts a mixture of monuments that reflect the city's historical past relative to both the Confederacy and the civil rights movement. The racialized history and geography of the city influences where students spend their time off campus: White students tend to frequent downtown spaces while Black students tend to travel further from campus where they feel safer. Within the past few years, there has been racial tension stemming from two separate incidents where local law enforcement shot unarmed Black men. These incidents have led to occasional protests and feelings of mistrust between Black residents and law enforcement.

On campus, the SU administration has discussed increased racial unrest among students. Students who belong to the Black Student Union have vocalized concerns about the lack of faculty of color and how these faculty do not mirror the growing number of students of color. Most recently, tensions spiked when a White faculty member called campus security when they noticed a Black student laying in the quad late at night who seemed "out of place." These campus concerns inspired SU to hire a social justice educator to work in their diversity office that serves all students regardless of their cultural background. In light of recent events, the administration asked the new staff member to develop and facilitate workshops and structured conversations on campus as part of an "embrace differences" campus initiative because there are currently no diversity requirements as part of the general education curriculum. The first program they have been asked to develop, facilitate, and assess is an optional four-part dialogue series about race and social perceptions.

Given the context described, race is the most salient social identity given the explicit attention on racial tensions and the racial composition of the student body. Because SU is located in a region of the country that memorializes both the Confederacy and the civil rights movement, it is highly likely that students on campus have prior knowledge about race, the country's racial history, and how race influences social interactions in contemporary society. When developing a dialogue series, students who are distressed by racial inequalities on campus and in the local community, passionate about racial justice, or uncertain yet interested in learning more may be more motivated to attend this optional dialogue series. It also seems likely that students who view race ambivalently or feel threatened by racially explicit conversations will be less motivated to attend. As a result, the dialogue series may attract students with both strong feelings and thoughts as well as students looking to enhance their understanding of race. Because SU does not have a general education curriculum that focuses on differences, specifically race and racial differences, it is likely that students will come to the dialogue series without a common language but with an independently developed understanding of race. Therefore, all of these elements seem most relevant for the social justice educator developing this dialogue series.

Handout 1.1
Reflecting on Contextual Influences:
Yourself, the Educator

1. Identify your social identities and circle those that you believe are most salient to this workshop or structured conversation.

   a. Race:

   b. Ethnicity:

   c. Sex:

   d. Gender:

   e. Sexual orientation:

   f. Ability status:

   g. Religion or faith:

   h. Social class:

   i. Other:

   j. Other:

2. How do you enact your most salient social identities?

3. How might your salient social identities impact your facilitation?

Reflecting on Contextual Influences:
Student and Environmental Influences

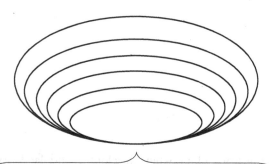

When considering environmental influences:
7. How might *educational* factors, including prior content covered, existing group dynamics, and the duration of the experience, shape the workshop or structured conversation?

When considering student influences:
4. What *demographics* are present among the students that might be most relevant to the workshop or structured conversation?

8. What recent *campus* events or potential campus climate concerns might different students have that are relevant to how they perceive or experience the workshop or structured conversation?

5. What prior *knowledge* or relevant formal or informal education experiences have these students shared prior to this workshop or structured conversation, and how might they shape how different students engage the experience?

9. What relevant recent *off-campus* issues at the local, state, or national levels might influence different students' perceptions of, or experience during, the workshop or structured conversation?

6. What might *motivate* different students to attend or fully participate in this workshop or structured conversation, and how might that shape the nature of their participation?

CHAPTER 2

Theories and Conceptual Frameworks

Imagine for a moment that you are developing a 2-hour workshop for international students to learn about social inequality in the United States. As you plan the workshop based on the relevant contextual influences, how do you think about the workshop content related to your students? Would it make sense to use a conceptual framework about systemic power, privilege, and oppression for students who are not familiar with these concepts in the United States? Alternatively, should you use developmental theories to help students understand their own social identities and experiences with social inequality? Given who you are and what you value, what do *you* believe is most important, and how might that align with the needs of these students?

To answer these questions, theoretical and conceptual frameworks are helpful to design and facilitate the experience. Theories and conceptual frameworks are ways to organize the approach to social justice education. Bonilla et al. (2012) use the metaphor of a lens to describe how theoretical and conceptual frameworks influence social justice educators' work. Lenses literally change perception, shaping the way things appear and what is actually seen as a result. Lenses allow educators to sharpen their focus, see things in greater detail, and view their surroundings with greater precision. However, lenses can increase the focus on some objects at the expense of others, and thus can restrict educators' vision. Therefore, social justice educators should be intentional about which theories and conceptual frameworks they adopt because of how they can alter what educators see and assume to be true for their students.

Having a thoughtful understanding of the contextual influences discussed in chapter 1 should directly inform which theories and conceptual frameworks

educators adopt when developing and facilitating a social justice education workshop or structured conversation. Each theory and conceptual framework is grounded in different beliefs and assumptions about human differences and social inequality, including the ways students make sense of their social reality. Sometimes, it may be helpful to use multiple lenses together to enhance student learning (Bonilla et al., 2012). While multiple theories and conceptual frameworks exist, four are introduced that are broadly useful for many of the workshops and structured conversations educators may develop and facilitate (see Figure 2.1). What follows is a *brief* review of each theory and conceptual framework, followed by a discussion of how they are useful when developing educational experiences. Please refer to the original scholarship to learn more beyond this overview.

Developmental Model of Intercultural Sensitivity

Milton Bennett's (2013) developmental model of intercultural sensitivity (DMIS) examines how individuals navigate cultural differences. This developmental theory focuses on helping individuals successfully develop knowledge and skills to acknowledge, understand, and embrace cultural differences for the purpose of effective intercultural interaction. The model describes how students develop across six different stages as they shift from an ethnocentric to ethnorelative worldview. These six stages include denial, defense, minimization, acceptance, adaptation, and integration.

The first three stages of denial, defense, and minimization are associated with an ethnocentric worldview

FIGURE 2.1. Selected theories and conceptual frameworks for social justice education.

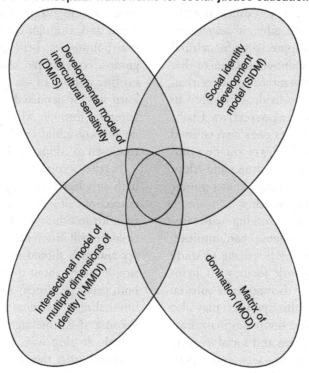

where one's own culture is always central to how they view others. A person in *denial* believes that one's own culture is the only legitimate culture. As a result, the existence of other cultures, and the value they bring, are "denied." In *defense*, a person acknowledges other cultures; however, they will still maintain that one's own culture is the most valuable culture. In the end, they view all other cultures as inferior to their own. Therefore, a White person in defense might acknowledge aspects of Black culture, such as jazz music, yet deem it inferior. However, someone in *minimization* does not view their culture as superior, but instead sees their culture as normative and universal. Therefore, instead of viewing cultural differences as inferior, individuals simply view cultural differences as variations of their own culture.

Sometimes these ethnocentric stages may seem too similar, so consider the example of race through the lens of a White person in these stages. A White person in denial would not recognize other racial communities at all. Once in defense, a White person may acknowledge other racial cultures but deem them inferior. If considering cultural contributions to music, they may acknowledge the cultural contributions of Black people to jazz music; however, they may still

argue that traditional classical music, primarily developed by White Europeans, is superior. However, this same White person in minimization may not view White culture as superior to Black culture. Instead, they would suggest that elements of Black culture are variations of White culture. For example, this White person may suggest that Black people's contributions of jazz music are simply variations of classical music developed by European Whites.

As someone progresses through ethnocentric stages of development, they maintain a view of their culture as "normative" or "better" than cultures different from their own, with varying degrees of negative views toward difference. However, someone in one of the ethnocentric stages may not consciously see themselves as a cultural being with a distinct cultural background. Therefore, how they see (or do not see) themselves contributes to a simplistic view of their own cultural position relative to others.

The last three stages of acceptance, adaptation, and integration are associated with an ethnorelative worldview. All three stages are marked with an individual who is able to see themselves and others as cultural beings of equal value and worth. A person in *acceptance* believes their own culture is one among many other complex cultures that deserve equal value. In this stage, cultural differences are truly just different without judgement toward one or the other. In *adaptation*, a person may develop a deeper appreciation for cultural differences and empathy for cultural experiences that help them take seriously different perspectives than their own. In this stage, the individual literally can adapt their view to consider other perspectives. Lastly, a person in *integration* experiences one's own cultural background as flexible and fluid. This orientation supports their ability to weave among cultures and adopt a more complex view of one's cultural self as a mosaic of various cultural values and approaches.

DMIS can be useful when working with students who come from homogenous communities, are international students, or are preparing to study abroad. Because this framework focuses on helping students become aware of themselves as cultural beings and value differences, this approach may also be useful for students who have limited or inaccurate knowledge of cultural differences and social identity groups. Understanding how people view and experience cultural differences offers valuable insight into ways to promote self-exploration and an appreciation of difference that is foundational to social justice education.

Social Identity Development Model

Rita Hardiman and Bailey Jackson's (1997) social identity development model (SIDM) examines how individuals develop a sense of their social identity directly associated with their experiences of privilege and oppression. While numerous other developmental theories exist specific to various social identities (see Torres, 2011, for a comprehensive list), this model considers how individuals psychologically understand social power across different manifestations of privileged and oppressed social identity groups. The purpose of this model is to support students as they develop knowledge, awareness, and skills to move away from internalized superiority and inferiority and move toward social action. SIDM consists of five developmental stages that include naïve/no social consciousness, acceptance, resistance, redefinition, and internalization.

In the first stage, *naïve/no social consciousness*, people have no knowledge or preconceived notions about the norms and expectations of their social identity group memberships. People simply experience the world and, through their experiences, begin to learn the boundaries between different social identity groups. For example, children are not born with pre-existing notions of sex and gender. However, children learn specific gendered scripts for acting masculine or feminine through what people and institutions may do and say. Children also learn which scripts they are supposed to adopt for themselves.

In the second stage of *acceptance*, members of both privileged and oppressed groups internalize the dominant culture's values and beliefs as normative and superior to other social identity groups. For example, children will internalize messages that boys should not cry and girls should not display assertive behavior as simple truths about the world. However, members of both privileged (men) and oppressed (women) groups internalize these same messages about one another. Because these messages are viewed as truths, individuals develop ways to rationalize any instances of inequality that they perceive. For example, if a boy's peers make fun of him for crying, he may rationalize it as deserved because boys are not supposed to cry, and believe he should only display emotions that are associated with strength and dominance.

The third stage of *resistance* is when members of both privileged and oppressed groups begin to question values and beliefs assumed to be normative or superior. Because individuals begin to question these elements of the status quo, they also begin to realize and reject systems of inequality, privilege, and oppression. At this stage of development, members of privileged and oppressed groups begin to have differing experiences as they examine their experiences with social power in society. People from privileged groups begin exploring their role in perpetuating oppression, which can often lead to strong emotional responses of guilt and shame. Simultaneously, people from oppressed groups become skilled in identifying the presence of discrimination and oppression in their lives, which may lead to strong emotional responses of frustration and anger. Emotional responses from both groups are useful at the resistance stage. Emotions cultivate an advanced conceptual and empathetic understanding of oppression and its impact on members of both privileged and oppressed groups.

When people from both privileged and oppressed groups enter the fourth stage of *redefinition*, they attempt to create a new sense of self based on their newfound ability to see and reject systems of inequality and related beliefs of superiority or inferiority. People from privileged groups begin to relearn aspects of their dominant identities in ways that affirm their strengths while simultaneously acknowledging their role in oppression. For example, cisgender men might find ways to embrace athleticism without problematic elements of toxic masculinity while also affirming women who embrace athleticism. Meanwhile, people experiencing oppression shift away from an identity defined in opposition to people with privilege and instead identify with people from their own social identity groups on their own terms. For example, a woman may reject binary notions of masculinity and femininity and embrace a combination of elements as part of their identity. This aspect of reframing one's identity is a significant part of creating a supportive, nurturing, and culturally affirming space for oneself and others with whom they interact.

In the fifth stage of *internalization*, people from both privileged and oppressed groups strive to transform their awareness of systems of inequality, privilege, and oppression into their life through action. People from privileged groups strive to act as allies for social change and integrate socially just habits into their daily lives. For example, cisgender people may incorporate their awareness of gender identity and expression by always introducing themselves along with their gender pronouns. People from oppressed groups may engage in similar behavior; however, they may also integrate a sense of pride and self-esteem into their interactions with others as they renegotiate their relationships with and within society. For example, cisgender women may find ways to embrace aspects of femininity on their own terms, divorced from socialized assumptions and expectations that women ought to perform femininity a specific way.

SIDM offers a useful approach to cultivate knowledge, awareness, and skills grounded in an understanding of social power manifested in privileged and oppressed social identity groups. This model's ability to acknowledge and affirm cognitive and emotional challenges associated with learning and unlearning aspects of identity are useful for educators interested in cultivating an educational experience that embraces emotional intelligence. This approach may be useful with students who will be together over an extended period of time, receive individualized mentorship, or

have a strong desire for intrapersonal development. Students who are in the earlier stages of this model may benefit from this in combination with DMIS as students shift from an ethnocentric stance into an awareness of how systems of privilege and oppression perpetuate and reward ethnocentrism.

Matrix of Domination

Patricia Hill Collins's (2009) matrix of domination (MOD) framework provides a sociological examination regarding how social identity categories (e.g., social class) are connected to forms of oppression (e.g., classism). Unlike other frameworks about privilege and oppression, Collins's approach acknowledges how multiple manifestations of oppression and privilege interconnect to maintain one another at the individual, institutional, and cultural levels. Therefore, this framework helps students develop knowledge and awareness about the existence of privilege and oppression broadly and with respect to multiple social identity categories through the similarities, differences, and points of connection among different social identities.

Because this framework highlights how social identity groups are privileged and oppressed across multiple social identity categories, it provides an opportunity to consider similarities among members of different privileged groups and oppressed groups, respectively. For example, both cisgender men and heterosexuals experience privilege, while lesbians, gays, and bisexuals all experience oppression. Therefore, this framework helps students to examine how a gay, cisgender man simultaneously experiences privilege related to gender and oppression related to sexuality. As such, this framework can help students consider the ways that individuals who are gay and transgender face similar oppressions with respect to their privileged counterparts (i.e., heterosexuals, cisgender men). Overall, it illustrates how multiple forms of oppression interconnect with commonalities and differences related to how privileged and oppressed groups are perpetuated.

The MOD framework is useful to facilitate reflection on macro-level issues of inequality and connect them to personal experiences of privilege and oppression. This approach may be useful for students who seek a language and framework to describe experiences of inequality, or who may benefit from a stronger emphasis on knowledge development. Because SIDM also shares a focus on systems of privilege and oppression, educators can integrate both of these frameworks together.

Intersectional Model of Multiple Dimensions of Identity

Susan Jones, Elise Abes, and Stephen Quaye's intersectional model of multiple dimensions of identity (I-MMDI; see Jones & Abes, 2013) is another conceptual framework that synthesizes a sociological view of social power with a psychological view of individual development. Similar to Collins's MOD framework, this framework explores how individuals experience their lives through the simultaneous and intersecting social identities they experience. This model does not examine individual development through discrete stages like DMIS and SIDM. Instead, I-MMDI examines the relationship between how individuals see themselves and others through the multiple social identities they hold within intersecting systems of privilege and oppression.

This model explains how individuals make sense of reality through a five-part conceptual framework including the macro context, multiple social identities, identity salience, meaning-making filter, and core. The macro context refers to structural and institutional systems of privilege and oppression (e.g., ableism, heterosexism) that envelops all aspects of a person's lived experience. Within this macro context exist individuals with multiple social identities (e.g., able-bodied, person with a disability, bisexual, heterosexual) that intersect and shape how a person experiences the world. These two parts are similar to Collins's (2009) MOD framework.

The notion of identity salience refers to a person's most prevalent social identities given their multiple social identities within the macro context in which they live. In some cases, a person may see a single social identity as more salient than other social identities. For example, a person who identifies as both able-bodied and bisexual may find their sexuality to be more salient than their ability status given the nature of their experiences relative to both social identities. In other cases, a person may experience multiple identities as deeply intertwined, or intersectional, and collectively salient relative to their other social identities. For example, a person who identifies as a lesbian transgender woman

may find their gender and sexual identities mutually salient as they navigate their daily life. Additionally, individuals who identify as multiracial may find their racial identity to be most salient as a single multiracial identity or as racially intersectional between their multiple racial identities. However, identity salience can change given a person's life experiences and interactions with the macro context.

For example, I (Scott) identify as a White, middle-class man who was born into a working-class family. When I create and facilitate workshops on college campuses, my White racial identity is most salient since I tend to focus on issues of race. However, when I am spending time with my parents, my sister, and her kids, who are all White, my racial identity becomes less salient. Instead, my middle-class identity becomes more salient in this context because social class differences between us feel more apparent to me.

The macro context, social identities, and identity salience collectively describe the way a person interacts with their external environment that shapes how they see and understand themselves. At times, the macro context may play out consistently in various professional, social, and personal spaces in which educators exist.

For example, I (Roger) identify as a Latinx, straight man of middle-class background. Further, I was raised Catholic but have not considered myself religiously affiliated since my undergraduate college days. However, my religious social identity is salient in my professional life, having spent the last 15 years of my career working in religiously affiliated institutions with a student body that is significantly religiously affiliated. I select and develop programs knowing what the latest research says about how traditional college-aged students view religion. I consistently give attention to religion, remembering my own spiritual journey and the questions and hard decisions I grappled with. I also have been able to use my own experience to effectively reach nonaffiliated students and create space for atheists, agnostics, or free thinkers to feel safe in sharing their stories in a supportive space.

As a professional who also helps develop and lead LGBT+ trainings and educational workshops and programs, I am mindful of the ways being straight limits my expertise. Being the father of a gay child also helps me contribute a unique perspective and set of experiences into the programs I develop. The saliency of these social identities are regular reminders to use my privilege to reinforce my commitment to these issues, to communicate my limits, and to let folks know I always have more to learn, which helps build trust and stronger relationships with students.

The final two parts of the I-MMDI framework, the meaning-making filter and the core, make clear that the salient social identities given the macro context in which one lives influence the ways in which they make meaning of their lives and how they view themselves. The meaning-making filter acts as an intrapersonal lens through which a person understands the macro context and their multiple social identities given which social identity (or identities) are most salient. For example, if a student identifies as a Christian cisgender woman, her religious identity may be most salient and shape how she views her gendered experiences in ways that minimize gender inequality and sexism. However, a different student who identifies as a Jewish cisgender man may make meaning of his collective experiences and argue that sexism is not a problem, and instead argue that religious discrimination is a more pressing issue that contributes to social inequality. All of a person's lived experiences go through this filter to inform the core, or how they ultimately see themselves and the world. Therefore, in the previously shared examples, a Christian cisgender woman or a Jewish cisgender man can both, possibly, not view their gender identity as significant in their lives and also dismiss the role of gender and sexism in the world given how they have made meaning of their experiences.

I-MMDI is useful for understanding and engaging the diverse perspectives and experiences students have regarding issues of diversity and social justice. This approach may be useful for students who have intersectional salient social identities or have trouble understanding the simultaneous experience of privilege and oppression from their social identities. Advanced students who seek a more complex, layered, and multi-identity focus could also benefit from the educational experiences designed through this model.

Using These Frameworks as a Starting Point

The four frameworks described here reflect an intentional selection among numerous relevant conceptual and developmental theories. Readers may notice that these frameworks are not specific to any social identity and therefore can apply to a broad range of students. These frameworks were chosen based on the belief that social identities matter within the broader context

of social power. In this way, it may be noticeable which frameworks dominate our approach to this work. Further, the intentional choices illustrate how various theoretical and conceptual frameworks focus on different aspects when supporting student learning. Considering student development on a longer continuum, these lenses range from developing an awareness of cultural difference (DMIS), cultural differences connected to social power (SIDM), institutionalized social power (MOD), or social identity differences connected to institutionalized social power (I-MMDI).

There are numerous theories and frameworks that can be useful for developing educational workshops and structured conversations related to exploring culture, celebrating diversity, and working for social justice. This selection of suggested frameworks does not reflect a belief that these approaches are the only one's worth knowing, or that they are superior to others. Instead, these approaches provide educators a useful launching point for developing curricula for workshops and structured conversations guided by the approach to social justice education discussed in this book. Therefore, consider these four frameworks as useful starting points that can be expanded on as knowledge and experience are developed. Indeed, it may be critical to draw on additional theories and conceptual frameworks depending on the specific students an educator encounters and the contextual influences identified as relevant (see Torres, 2011, for a thorough categorization of specific theories relative to multiple social identities).

Considering Your Default Theory or Conceptual Framework(s)

Before educators think about which frameworks are most appropriate to guide the development and facilitation of a workshop or structured conversation, it is imperative to make explicit our "default lens," which will shape this approach to social justice education. Because we, the educators, are a contextual influence to consider prior to developing and facilitating a curriculum (see chapter 1), we must consider our default lens about student development and the nature of society when we set out to educate our students. Our default lens may be the result of factors that include our education, social identities, and the context where we work.

For example, I (Roger) strongly consider the MOD framework to be my default lens because of my education, and, more importantly, because of my lived experience. I see systems everywhere and in most settings. That said, I find myself intentionally walking through Bennett's DMIS as a way to remind myself that each individual is on a journey of awareness and those with privilege are often unconscious of their own privilege and its impact on others.

I (Scott) use SIDM as my default lens because my training in social work makes me partial to developmental theories. Further, my developmental journey of coming to terms with my privileged and oppressed experiences as a non-Christian, White cisgender male from a working-class family helped me empathize with how privilege and oppression looked from identities different from my own (e.g., Christians, people of color, cisgender women, transgender people, and middle-class people). Therefore, because the social identity development lens helped me make sense of my own life and mirrored my personal journey, I find it intuitive, and it is a useful place where I tend to begin my work. While I use the other frameworks in my work often, I tend to think about workshops and structured conversations from this lens unless I consciously decide to adopt a different lens.

From these examples, it becomes clear that it is not inherently problematic to have a default lens. However, it is important that we are aware of our default lens so that we can reflect on how that lens influences the development and facilitation of each educational experience.

Before developing a social justice education workshop or structured conversation, take a moment to reflect on the frameworks that primarily guide your work. Additionally, reflect on which frameworks seem most relevant given the contextual influences you previously identified will impact student learning. Consider the following questions:

Your "default" theories or conceptual frameworks

- Which theories or conceptual frameworks resonate the most with you and your approach to social justice education?
- How might your social identities and related experiences influence the theories or conceptual frameworks that you default to using in this work?

The most relevant default theories or conceptual frameworks

- Which theories or conceptual frameworks seem most useful given what you know about the students, specifically related to the following:
  o Demographics
  o Prior knowledge
  o Motivation to participate
- Which theories or conceptual frameworks seem most useful given what you know about the environment, specifically related to the following:
  o Expectations from stakeholders for the workshop or structured conversation
  o Amount of time you have for the workshop or structured conversation
  o Relevant issues on campus or the broader social environment that may be pressing on students

Western College

An introductory workshop for first-year students in the residence halls about sex and gender would benefit from the DMIS framework. DMIS provides insight to how students evolve to understand and accept different cultures, including different ways of performing gender that contradict a binary view of gender and gender expression. Given how some students struggle to understand the purpose and benefits of all-gender housing, their dissonance likely stems from an unexamined perspective on their own sex and gender expression. DMIS offers insights into students who come from homogenous backgrounds, where individuals perform gender in traditional ways that closely align to rigid views of maleness versus femaleness. Using DMIS to examine students' prior knowledge of sex and gender can help challenge exclusionary views and promote interest in the topic that can leverage the local feminist bookstore. The residence hall context further underscores the value of using a framework that promotes understanding and acceptance in students' home on campus.

It is also important to remember that student resident advisers will be developing and facilitating this workshop. Therefore, the framework needs to be simple enough for student staff to use given their level of training on the topic. Additionally, DMIS aligns with one of the goals for living on campus: to learn about others and explore different ways of being. DMIS acknowledges and encourages exploration of different ways of being in order to adopt a sense of self that incorporates multiple cultural elements into one's own identity.

Southeastern University

Given the expectation for the new social justice educator to create a racial dialogue series, the MOD framework would be useful to examine systems of privilege and oppression in a macro context that can be applied to students' personal experiences. Multiple aspects of the environment support the value of this framework. The racialized realities that exist in the local community, such as the racially segregated neighborhoods, historical monuments to the Confederacy and the civil rights movement, and police shootings, would provide ample content for students to discuss in these dialogues. Additionally, the racial demographics of the student body relative to the local city, and the places where students choose to spend their time, would provide useful material for a race-based dialogue series that examines students' realities in the context of macro-level structures of racial oppression and White privilege. Lastly, the relatively recent campus incident where a White faculty member called campus security on a Black student would be useful to examine through a historical and structural analysis of racial power in the United States.

There are also student factors that support the use of the MOD framework. Given how students do not have a general education requirement on diversity, it is unlikely they share a common language to discuss the racial incidents on campus or the racialized realities of their broader environment. In addition, the dialogue series would most likely attract students with strong feelings and perspectives about race, as well as students beginning to think about racial issues. Therefore, the MOD framework could provide a common language around race, power, privilege, and oppression to examine race. Such a focus could benefit students learning this content for the first time while also providing opportunities for students to continue mastering this content and sharpen their understanding with further evidence.

The other theories and conceptual frameworks do not seem as useful given these contextual influences. DMIS, which focuses on accommodating different cultural perspectives and experiences, would not be appropriate given that the students likely to attend the dialogue series are not demonstrating an inability to engage people different from themselves. SIDM, which focuses on developing a personal understanding of one's privileged or oppressed identity, seems to be more useful after a foundational understanding of race and racial power has been developed among students who are less likely to share a language about social power in the first place. I-MMDI, which focuses on interlocking matrices of privilege and oppression through various social identities, would similarly be more useful with a foundational understanding among students and an expectation to focus beyond race for this dialogue series. However, I-MMDI might be a useful lens to partner with a future dialogue series for students who participated in this first dialogue series explicitly on race.

Handout 2.1
Reflecting on Theories and Conceptual Frameworks
Relative to Contextual Influences

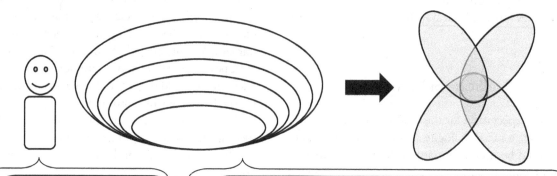

1. Which theories or conceptual frameworks resonate the most with you and your approach to social justice education?

2. How might your social identities and related experiences influence the theories or conceptual frameworks that you default to using in this work?

3. Which theories or conceptual frameworks seem useful given what you know about the students, specifically related to the following:

   a. Demographics

   b. Prior knowledge

   c. Motivation to participate

4. Which theories or conceptual frameworks seem useful given the environment, specifically related to the following:

   a. Expectations from stakeholders for the workshop or structured conversation

   b. Amount of time you have for the workshop or structured conversation

   c. Relevant issues on campus or from the broader social environment that may be pressing on students

CHAPTER 3

Cultural Consciousness and Learning Outcomes

Educators may struggle when narrowing their learning goals because it is challenging to prioritize content areas over others. Indeed, it can feel difficult to create boundaries between content that educators see as deeply interconnected. Consider these questions:

- How does one teach about racial differences across communities without also teaching the history of racism and the creation of race as a social construction?
- How can one develop critical consciousness of how individuals benefit from privilege in their own lives without also learning how society institutionalizes social power to favor select groups?
- How might students learn skills for advocating against social inequality without reflecting on how they reinforce privilege and oppression in their own lives?
- How can educators convey the interconnected nature of oppression without talking about its multiple manifestations including (but not limited to) racism, sexism, classism, heterosexism, faithism, and ableism?

While it can feel challenging to prioritize the learning goals for social justice education, it is essential. Let us offer two reasons why. First, educators seldom have unlimited time for a workshop or structured conversation. Therefore, because a curriculum is always designed and facilitated under various constraints, time should be used intentionally with students. Second, if educators go into a workshop or structured conversation

without the learning goals that they expect students to achieve, they may not effectively assess the educational impact of the session (more on that in chapter 6).

It is important to note that prioritizing learning goals does not mean that educators value one content area over others. It simply means that educators are responsible for being aware of how to incorporate particular content areas to support student learning relative to their prioritized learning goals for a specific educational experience. In other words, prioritizing learning goals allows educators to make intentional choices around which content, both educator driven and student driven, should be used to enhance student learning.

The process of prioritizing learning goals is a two-step process. First, educators should consider what content areas are most important to address during the educational experience. Second, educators should take their identified content areas and formulate them into measurable learning outcomes. Doing so not only creates prioritized learning goals for the educational experience but also eases the process when selecting activities (see chapter 4) and assessing student learning (see chapter 6). Let us explore both parts of this process with respect to the literature.

Part 1: Identifying Content Areas

The broader literature on cultural or social justice competence is where many scholars discuss the various content areas relevant to social justice education (see Goodman, 2013; Pope et al., 2019; Rhodes, 2010;

Sue, 2001). Scholars describe the focus on developing individuals in this way as the development of cultural competence. The concept of cultural competence has gone by many names in different disciplines, including *cross-cultural competence* in counseling psychology (e.g., Sue et al., 1982), *intercultural competence* in intercultural communication (e.g., Bennett, 2009), and *multicultural competence* in higher education (e.g., Pope & Reynolds, 1997). While each field offers a slightly different definition, they all emphasize the development of individuals' knowledge, awareness, and behaviors for the purpose of interpersonal engagement across difference. *Knowledge* refers to a foundation of factual and conceptual information pertaining to social identity groups. *Awareness* refers to thoughts and attitudes that support critical reflection about oneself, others, and society. *Behaviors* refer to the capacity for engaging oneself, others, and institutions as a whole.

While the majority of the literature uses the phrase cultural *competence*, we prefer the label of cultural *consciousness*. For some, the notion of competence may imply a sense of finality (e.g., believing that "I am now competent"). However, one's development never ends because the world and the ways people engage difference constantly changes. Let us consider the example of social identity labels. Multiple social identity groups have used, claimed, or reclaimed different language for themselves over time. Within the lesbian, gay, and bisexual community, *queer* is simultaneously a historically pejorative term; an umbrella term for members of the lesbian, gay, or bisexual community; and sometimes as a label for individuals who do not claim being lesbian, gay, or bisexual. Similarly, popular understanding of gender identity and expression has evolved past the label of transgender and into categories such as genderqueer or gender nonconforming to make space for the various ways individuals identify themselves (Amherst College Queer Resource Center, n.d.). Intersectionality has also influenced labeling related to gender and race. For example, individuals once labeled as Hispanic have adopted different labels over time, including Latino (to incorporate other Spanish-speaking countries in Central and South America) and either Latin@ or Latinx (to shift away from the gendered aspect of the Spanish language) (Berastaín, 2017). In all of these examples, what society once believed to be culturally competent became outdated as our understanding of social identities and inclusivity evolved.

The idea of being culturally conscious builds on the notion of cultural humility. Cultural humility emphasizes a process for lifelong self-evaluation and self-critique with the goal of fixing power imbalances in society (Tervalon & Murray-Garcia, 1998). The notion that students and educators alike must continually learn is a constant theme throughout the social justice education literature (see Bell, Goodman, & Varghese, 2016; Freire, 2000; Harro, 2013; hooks, 1994). As Lee Ann Bell, Diane Goodman, and Rani Varghese (2016) discuss in detail, there are multiple reasons why one's learning must continue. Social identities shape the ways educators experience the world and therefore are constantly shaping what they know, how they feel, and their ability to interact with others. As they move through life, educators must continually examine their assumptions and biases, maintain and enhance their ability to interact with others similar to and different from themselves, and explore their emotions and associated reactions regarding social identity. Additionally, Bobbie Harro (2013) reminds educators that individuals are socialized with a specific understanding of themselves and others based on their social identities. Part of continual learning involves unlearning problematic views about group superiority and inferiority that may not be easily seen or acknowledged. bell hooks (1994) and Paulo Freire (2000) refer to this continual reflection on personal actions as *praxis*. Praxis is essential because it encourages educators to constantly examine the extent to which they are continually congruent in their knowledge, awareness, and behaviors in the pursuit of social justice. For these reasons, we will continue our discussion using the label cultural consciousness to emphasize the importance of continual growth and development for our students and ourselves.

While the three dimensions of cultural consciousness (knowledge, awareness, and behaviors) provide a foundation to think about content areas for student learning, these alone may not help educators prioritize learning goals. Tharp's (2015) cultural consciousness matrix (see Figure 3.1) is useful to focus beyond knowledge, awareness, and behaviors while still aligning with Bell's (2007) social justice education framework, discussed previously in the introduction of this book. Let us examine each dimension of this model and illustrate how they contribute collectively to content areas for social justice education.

FIGURE 3.1. Cultural consciousness matrix.

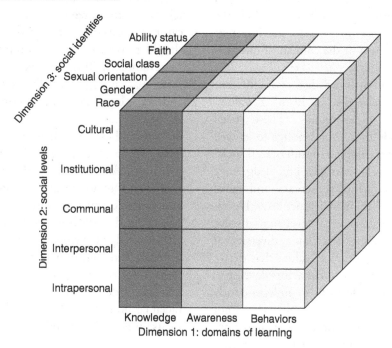

Dimension 1: Domains of Learning

The first dimension considers different domains of development discussed in the broader cultural competence literature, including knowledge, awareness, and behaviors. Again, knowledge refers to factual and conceptual information pertaining to social identity groups, awareness refers to the internalization of values that result in specific dispositions and critical reflection, and behaviors refers to having the capacity for action. One or more of these domains of learning may be essential to focus on given the theories or conceptual frameworks used to develop and facilitate any given social justice education workshop or structured conversation. Given how educators interpret the contextual factors using the different theories or conceptual frameworks, the emphasis of the workshop or structured conversation may lean more heavily toward a single domain. For example, a workshop guided by Collins's (2009) MOD framework may prioritize knowledge about systems of oppression across multiple social identities. However, a structured conversation guided by Bennett's (2013) development model of intercultural sensitivity may prioritize awareness of one's own social identities that educators supplement with knowledge about social identity differences and behaviors for dialoguing across difference.

Dimension 2: Social Levels

The second dimension highlights different social levels of human influence and interaction where educators can further nuance the domains of learning. The five social levels are an adaption of Derald Wing Sue's (2001) model that discusses four foci specific to helping professionals, including individual, professional, organization, and society. Inspired by Urie Bronfenbrenner's (1979) ecological systems theory, there are five levels of learning that range from the micro to the macro level. These five levels of learning include intrapersonal, interpersonal, communal, institutional, and cultural levels.

The intrapersonal level considers content specific to oneself. This level might include knowledge of *one's own* social identities, awareness of *one's own* personal biases, and behaviors for *self*-reflection. Within the intrapersonal level, the object of learning is oneself. Relatedly, the interpersonal level of learning considers content areas specific to interactions *between* oneself and other individuals. These other individuals can be from either similar or different social identity groups as oneself. Interpersonal content areas may include knowledge about how social interactions *between* racial groups are shaped by history, awareness about how one's social identity-based values manifest in *interactions* with people different from themselves, and behaviors to actively listen *across* difference. While the intrapersonal level focuses on oneself, the interpersonal level focuses on them in the context of interacting with others.

The communal level acknowledges that different social identity groups have distinct histories, values, and behaviors worth understanding. These social identity groups include those one belongs to as well as those to which others belong. Consider racial social identity communities as an example; knowledge may include the history of White supremacy and racial subjugation of people of color in distinct ways. Developing awareness at the communal level may involve valuing diversity (including one's own diversity of social identities) or being aware of values that derive from one's social identity groups. Behaviors developed within this level can include skills to independently learn about people different from oneself, such as not defaulting to ask people of color about their history but instead learning how to intentionally and respectfully cultivate understanding about social identity communities.

The institutional level examines content related to the way society is structured. This level of learning looks beyond individuals or groups and focuses on social institutions, such as government, health care, or education. The institutional level makes explicit that institutional policies and practices are separate from the individuals who participate in these institutions. Content areas within the institutional level might examine knowledge about how sexism manifests within schools, awareness of how sexist policies and practices in school affect cisgender women and transgender students, and behaviors to challenge sexist policies and practices within schools.

The final level, the cultural level, examines content regarding the broader values and norms within society. Different from the institutional level, the cultural level involves the less tangible or readily apparent aspects of society because it may feel normal or appear to be "just the way things are." Knowledge may involve understanding that social identity categories are social constructions used to control social identity groups. Awareness may include valuing social justice and different ways of treating social identity groups. Behaviors can include skills to challenge assumptions about what is normative in order to consider more socially just alternatives.

Distinguishing among five different social levels relative to the three domains of learning allows educators to consider critically the specific content they should prioritize when grappling with broad topics. For example, a 90-minute workshop on race is a broad topic that could potentially entail all five social levels and three learning domains (see Table 3.1). A workshop about race can focus on one's intrapersonal development and examine their own racial experiences and biases while developing skills for ongoing racial self-reflection. Alternatively, a different workshop about race could focus solely on interpersonal behaviors and practice skills for cross-racial dialogue. Further still, a third workshop about race could focus solely on knowledge development across the cultural, institutional, and communal levels by examining race as a social construction, how it has been manifested into law over time, and the impact it has had on different racial communities. While all three workshops would focus on race, they all prioritize very different content.

Dimension 3: Social Identities

Just as learning domains and social levels can be specified about the broader topic of race, all social justice education topics can be considered relative to one or more social identity category. The third dimension of social identities makes explicit how content can be distinct relative to social identity categories (e.g., race), as well as social identities within those categories (e.g., Asian, Black, Latinx, White). This framework explicitly calls attention to race, gender, sexual orientation, social class, faith, and ability status; however, educators can consider other social identities as well. It is also important to acknowledge that the matrix presents social identities in this dimension as separate; however, educators can think about these social identities from an intersectional perspective as well.

This third dimension ensures that educators do not assume that all content is the same for all social identities. On the contrary, content will look different depending on which social identities are prioritized. Just as Table 3.1 provides an example of content with respect to race, the same holds true for other social identity categories. The history of racism is not the same as the history of heterosexism. The experience of racial oppression is not the same as the experience of sexual oppression. While privilege and oppression across multiple social identity groups have similarities, educators should not view them as the same.

TABLE 3.1. Example Content for a Race Workshop Relative to Social Levels and Learning Domains

	Knowledge	*Awareness*	*Behaviors*
Cultural	Knowledge about concepts of race, racial privilege, and racial oppression	Awareness of socially just values that challenge racial privilege and oppression	Skills that help identify racial inequality in society
Institutional	Knowledge about how racial privilege and oppression is historically and contemporarily manifested in law	Awareness of different legal policies and practices that could advance racial justice	Skills to advocate for racially just changes to legal policies and practices
Communal	Knowledge about racial identities and experiences different from one's own racial identity	Awareness of racial values and traditions different from one's own racial identity	Skills to independently learn about racial communities different from one's own racial community
Interpersonal	Knowledge about historical and contemporary Black and White relations	Awareness of how one's racial values and beliefs influence interracial relationships	Skills to dialogue with individuals from different racial groups
Intrapersonal	Knowledge about one's own racial identity and racial experiences	Awareness of one's own racial biases	Skills to critically examine one's own racial experiences and biases

Consider the broad topics of race and sexual orientation. While racial oppression and sexual oppression bestow privilege on Whites and heterosexuals respectively, privilege manifests itself distinctively for each group. Members of racially privileged groups are typically identified based on physical characteristics associated with race, including skin color, facial features, and hair texture. However, heterosexuals do not share similar physical features. Therefore, privilege was conferred to Whites based on physical characteristics while heterosexuals received privilege based on sexual behavior. While both racism and heterosexism have been argued using pseudoscientific beliefs (Ordover, 2003; Winfield, 2007) and religious reasoning (Kivel, 2013), racism was codified through "one-drop" laws to determine racial group memberships that were linked to one's legal standing (Jordan, 2014), and heterosexism was codified through laws that criminalized same-sex behaviors (Weinmeyer, 2014).

Because of these differences, educators seldom prioritize multiple social identities with respect to multiple social levels and learning domains. However, if educators want to delve into a select few social levels

or learning domains, it could provide more time to examine content across multiple social identities. For example, on one hand, an educator might prioritize intrapersonal knowledge and awareness with respect to multiple social identities. On the other hand, an educator might focus on interpersonal behaviors for intergroup dialogue and teach how interactions differ across social identity groups. Just as content areas are more specific based on social levels and learning domains, social identities help educators specify the learning they wish to prioritize with their students.

It is important for educators to consider all three dimensions of the cultural consciousness matrix when prioritizing content areas for social justice workshops and structured conversations. Educators can begin the prioritization process by looking at the grid and marking those squares that are most essential given the contextual influences and theories or conceptual frameworks previously identified in the planning process. Once educators identify which content areas are most essential, they can develop concrete learning outcomes that will guide the selection of activities and approaches to learning assessment (discussed in chapters 4 and 6). First, let us discuss how to write learning outcomes using the cultural consciousness matrix.

Part 2: Transforming Content Areas Into Learning Outcomes

Educators can cultivate significant learning among students when developing educational experiences with the end goal in mind, or what L. Dee Fink (2013) terms *backward design*. In addition to being intentional about social justice education content because of its complexity, social justice educators must also establish learning outcomes. The establishment of learning outcomes helps not only educators stay focused when developing and facilitating workshops and structured conversations but also students guide their learning (Bell, Goodman, & Ouellett, 2016). Therefore, transforming identified content areas into learning outcomes is an important step when putting together a social justice workshop or structured conversation.

While there are many definitions (Keeling et al., 2008; Maki, 2010; Suskie, 2009; Walvoord, 2010), a *learning outcome* is simply a specific and measurable statement regarding what a student will know or be able to do after completing an education experience. Unlike the content areas discussed, a learning outcome specifies with greater precision what the focus of learning will be and the extent to which students ought to demonstrate mastery. Learning outcomes make explicit what learning will occur and provide insight for how educators can assess student learning (more on this in chapter 6).

There are three parts to a learning outcome statement: the audience, the condition, and the behavior. The *audience* refers to the students who should demonstrate learning. For example, the audience can be all students, student employees, or first-year students who participate in a structured dialogue. The *condition* refers to the specific experience students will complete that supports learning. For example, conditions can be completing a 3-hour training, participating in at least two workshops, or attending a structured dialogue. Lastly, the *behavior* refers to the specific content that students will learn as well as the extent educators expect students to learn it. As previously

discussed regarding the learning domains within the cultural consciousness matrix, behaviors refer to more than skills or actions. Examples of behaviors in a learning outcome statement may include students' ability to define *race* and *racism*, explain the relationship between privilege and oppression, or demonstrate intergroup dialogue skills when interacting with other students on campus. Collectively, the audience, condition, and behavior make explicit what will be learned (the behavior), by who (the audience), and as a result of what experience (the condition).

The trickiest part of writing learning outcomes is transforming the content area into a specific, learning-focused behavior. Peggy Maki (2010) provides educators with multiple best practices to consider when writing a learning outcome statement. Of her best practices, the following are essential when developing learning outcomes for a social justice workshop or structured conversation:

- Meaningful
- Tied to learning
- Written using action verbs
- Observable
- Measurable
- Written at an appropriate level
- Clear and concise

Learning outcomes should be *meaningful* relative to the educational purpose. Therefore, learning outcomes for social justice education should advance the broader aims of social justice education. However, they should also be *tied to learning* by describing what students will learn, not what educators will teach. A common pitfall is to write a learning outcome statement that focuses on what educators will do (teach about racism) instead of what students will be able to demonstrate based on their learning (define *racism* and explain how racism exists in U.S. history). Learning outcomes *written using action verbs* that emphasize what students will know or can do will help educators ensure their learning outcomes focus on student learning. Using the previous example, the verb "teach" clearly suggests the focus is on teaching, while the verbs "define" and "explain" suggest actions that students will be able to accomplish to demonstrate what they learned. Good action verbs that focus on student learning are essential and ensure that the learning outcomes are both *observable* and *measurable*, meaning that an educator can "see" when a student demonstrates learning through a specifically quantified or qualified way. For example, an educator can observe whether a student can define *racism* by asking them to define the term. Further, educators can measure the extent to which the student's definition is accurate by examining the quality of the definition.

Ensuring that learning outcomes are *written at an appropriate level* requires attention to what is a realistic accomplishment given what is known about the students and the educational context. For example, it would be unrealistic to expect first-year college students to compare systems of privilege and oppression across multiple social identity groups after completing an hour-long workshop. There is simply no way to teach all of the necessary content for students to demonstrate this level of learning. However, it is reasonable to expect first-year college students to define *privilege* and *oppression* and identify how they experience privilege and oppression in their lives within the same timeframe. Lastly, learning outcomes should be *clear and concise* so that educators can know with certainty what content they will cover, how they can assess learning, and therefore what the expectations for success are by simply reading the outcome statement.

Consider the following examples of learning outcomes:

1. All students who complete a structured dialogue on race and racism will have knowledge to discuss race-based topics.
2. All students who complete a structured dialogue on race and racism will be able to define *race* and *racism*.
3. All students who complete a structured dialogue on race and racism will be able to describe how historical racism is present in contemporary times.

The first learning outcome statement describes the broader content area to be covered and makes clear the focus is on knowledge. However, it is not clear what knowledge students should learn or what types of race-based topics educators expect students to be able to discuss. The second and third learning outcomes are clear and concise, explicitly stating the type of knowledge and race-based topics that educators

expect their students to learn. A review of the last two outcomes helps educators know that the structured dialogue needs to help students define *race* and *racism* and provide content about historical and present-day racism in order for students to be successful.

Before developing a social justice education workshop or structured conversation, identify which content areas should be the focus of the experience given both the theories or conceptual frameworks and contextual influences previously identified. Consider the following questions:

Prioritizing content areas

- Which domains of learning are most essential for the workshop or structured conversation?
- Which levels of learning are most essential for the workshop or structured conversation?
- What social identities are most essential to examine within the workshop or structured conversation?
- Using the matrix of cultural consciousness, which content areas across domains of learning, levels of learning, and social identities should be specifically focused on for the workshop or structured conversation?

Transforming content areas into learning outcomes

- For each content area identified, think about them related to some of Maki's (2010) best practices for learning outcomes. Specifically, consider the following:
  - What action verb best expresses the type of learning you expect (e.g., identify, demonstrate, compare)?
  - What would successful learning look like if you observed it?
  - How would you either quantify or qualify student learning to measure it?
  - What is the appropriate level for student learning given the students and the educational context?
- For each identified content area, write a specific learning outcome statement that delineates the audience, condition, and behavior using Maki's best practices as a guide.

Western College

The primary goals for this workshop involve exploring concepts related to sex and gender and encouraging thoughtful interactions among students. Therefore, the content areas for this workshop would focus on the knowledge domain at the cultural level, as well as the behavior domain at the interpersonal level, with specific attention to sex and gender. If we were to map these content areas onto a two-dimensional version of the matrix of cultural consciousness, it might appear as illustrated in Table 3.2.

The following is an example of how these three content areas could be transformed into learning outcome statements associated with each content area (listed in parenthesis).

Students who participate in the sex and gender workshop will be able to do the following:

1. Describe how gender expression relates to sex and gender (cultural knowledge).
2. Identify communication strategies that respectfully explore how students express gender (intrapersonal behavior).

This workshop has only two learning outcomes; however, these two outcomes entail a fair amount of conceptual content to help students understand the relationships among concepts of sex, gender, and gender expression that set the stage to explore how to respectfully interact with others related to their gender expression. Both outcomes focus on what students ought to learn related to "describing" concepts and "identifying" communication strategies to engage

others. Both learning outcomes are observable and measurable in different ways. The first outcome lends itself to a qualitative approach to assessment based on the quality of the description students provide. The second outcome, however, lends itself to a quantitative approach based on the ability to identify the correct response from a list with incorrect options. Assuming this workshop would last about 45 minutes, these outcomes are at an appropriate level given the minimal amount of time afforded for this workshop set to occur within a residence hall. Lastly, both outcome statements are clear and simple in what the expectation for learning is at the end of the workshop.

Southeastern University

Race as a social identity would be prioritized for this dialogue series. It would be useful for the first dialogue in this series to focus on the knowledge domain at the cultural, intrapersonal, and communal levels to create a foundation on which students can extend their examination of race. For example, this first dialogue could explore concepts of race, privilege, oppression, and racism and how these concepts manifest themselves in the lives of the students. Additionally, this first dialogue could prioritize intrapersonal and interpersonal behaviors to teach students skills to examine one's racial identity and for interacting across racial groups. These skills would be useful to prepare students to participate in future dialogues with more challenging content. If we were to map these content areas onto a two-dimensional version of the matrix of cultural consciousness, it might appear as illustrated in Table 3.3.

TABLE 3.2 Completed Matrix of Cultural Consciousness for the Sex and Gender Workshop at Western College

	Knowledge	Awareness	Behaviors
Cultural	X		
Institutional			
Communal			
Interpersonal			X
Intrapersonal			

TABLE 3.3 Completed Matrix of Cultural Consciousness for the First Racial Dialogue at Southeastern University

	Knowledge	Awareness	Behaviors
Cultural	X		
Institutional			
Communal	X		
Interpersonal			X
Intrapersonal	X		X

The following is an example of how these five content areas could be transformed into learning outcome statements associated with each content area (listed in parenthesis).

Students who participate in the first racial dialogue will be able to do the following:

1. Define concepts of *race, privilege, oppression,* and *racism* (cultural knowledge)
2. Describe how racial privilege and oppression influence the experience of racial groups in the United States (communal knowledge)
3. Demonstrate skills for self-reflection related to their racial identity (intrapersonal behavior)
4. Demonstrate intergroup dialogue skills of listening and suspending judgement (interpersonal behavior)
5. Describe how their racial identity experiences privilege or oppression (intrapersonal knowledge)

All five of these learning outcome statements are tied to student learning because they use verbs that articulate that students will "define," "describe," and "demonstrate" knowledge or skills. Further, the content areas for each learning outcome are stated in ways that are observable (defining concepts, demonstrating specific behaviors) and qualitatively measurable. For example, how well a student demonstrates intergroup dialogue skills could be qualified based on how well they listen and suspend judgement when interacting with their peers. Assuming this first dialogue would last about 90 minutes, these outcomes are at an appropriate level given the time constraints and the assumption that those students likely to attend will be eager to participate and bring some prior knowledge to the dialogue. Lastly, each outcome statement is clear and "to the point" about what should be accomplished by the time the first dialogue concludes.

Handout 3.1
Reflecting on Cultural Consciousness Content Areas and Learning Outcomes

1. Using the matrix of cultural consciousness to the right, place an "x" in the squares to indicate which content areas are most essential for this learning experience.

2. Why are these content areas most essential?

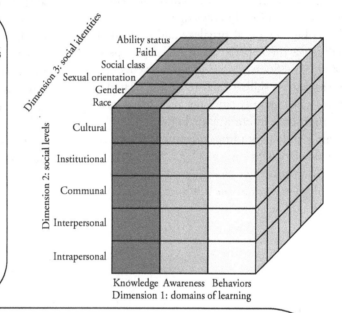

3. Transform each content area into a single learning outcome statement. Ensure each learning outcome statement includes all three parts and satisfies the seven best practices for writing learning outcomes:

_____ who _____
      (Audience)   (Condition)

will be able to:

Behavior a:

Behavior b:

Behavior c:

Behavior checklist:
- ☐ Meaningful
- ☐ Tied to learning
- ☐ Written using action verbs
- ☐ Observable
- ☐ Measurable
- ☐ Written at an appropriate level
- ☐ Clear and concise

CHAPTER 4

Pedagogical Considerations and Selecting Activities

"The academy is not paradise. But learning is a place where paradise can be created. The classroom, with all its limitations, remains a location of possibility. In that field of possibility we have the opportunity to labor for freedom, to demand of ourselves and our comrades, an openness of mind and heart that allows us to face reality even as we collectively imagine ways to move beyond boundaries, to transgress. This is education as the practice of freedom."

—bell hooks (1994, p. 207)

Lee Anne Bell (2007) describes social justice as "both a process and a goal" (p. 1). In her discussion of social justice, she is clear that educators who cultivate cultural consciousness must also engage in practices and processes that support a socially just world. In the quote that opens this chapter, bell hooks (1994) describes what a socially just educational process looks like. Specifically, educators should help students face their reality with both their minds and hearts in order to reimagine a more just world. However, educators must intentionally create a learning environment that allows for this type of learning to occur. Therefore, as educators consider ways to educate students on the learning outcomes identified in the previous chapter, they ought to do so with attention to their pedagogical approach, or their educational processes and practices.

Pedagogical Principles

Maurianne Adams (2016) identifies six pedagogical principles educators should incorporate into the development of social justice education curricula. These principles are important to remain congruent with the broader purpose and process of promoting social justice because "the pedagogical choices we make . . . are as important as the content we teach" (p. 27). While Adams's original principles are important to guide the development and facilitation of social justice education experiences, we provide a simplified version that includes five of these principles to help educators more easily incorporate all five into their practice. A simplified version of these five principles is visualized in Figure 4.1. Adhering to these simplified principles supports thoughtful educational practice while ensuring the educational experience itself models the essence of social justice. Let us explore what each principle means in practice as it relates to the curriculum design and facilitation of a workshop or structured conversation and then examine how they collectively inform the selection of activities.

Principle 1: Facilitate the Development of Knowledge, Awareness, and Behaviors

While chapter 3 discusses learning domains for cultural consciousness that include the development of students' knowledge, awareness, and behaviors, this principle highlights that social justice education should facilitate educational experiences that cultivate development across all three areas (Adams, 2016) even if they are not an explicit focus for the intended learning outcomes. As stated in the previous chapter, it is still permissible for educators to focus on content and subsequent learning outcomes relative to one or two

FIGURE 4.1. Visualization of principles for social justice education.

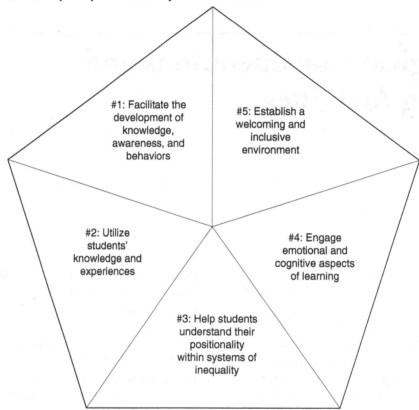

Note. Adams (2016).

of these learning domains. Indeed, developing cultural consciousness in one learning domain can theoretically contribute to the development of other dimensions (Tharp, 2015).

For example, consider a workshop that has a single learning outcome: "Students will define concepts of *race* and *racism.*" While this learning outcome focuses explicitly on the learning domain of knowledge, the teaching activities can also facilitate the development of awareness and skills. For instance, instead of solely lecturing on the concepts of *race* and *racism,* educators could incorporate time for reflection or discussion that helps students become aware of these concepts in their lives to help them understand these terms. Additionally, incorporating discussion helps students practice behaviors for discussing race with their peers. Even though the learning outcome focuses on knowledge development, educators can and should select activities to facilitate the development of all three learning domains.

Please allow us to share our reflections on a workshop activity called a privilege walk to illustrate how each principle helps in the process of planning an educational experience. This is a symbolic activity where an educator reads various statements and asks students to step forward each time the statement is true for them. The result positions students with greater privilege closer to the front and students with less privilege closer to the back, thus spatially recreating the social stratification that exists among students. I (Scott) have received requests to conduct privilege walks more than any other activity in my career.

So, to what extent does a privilege walk satisfy the first principle? A privilege walk can help develop students' knowledge about privilege given the statements that educators read aloud during the activity. Students' may also develop their awareness when they take note of their spatial position relative to their peers and challenge their own assumptions about their reality as normal or common. However, a privilege walk activity alone does not develop students' behaviors for social action. In order to develop students' behaviors, another activity would be necessary, such as a discussion activity where educators ask students to identify ways to challenge privilege and oppression.

Principle 2: Utilize Students' Knowledge and Experiences

For educators to help students develop knowledge, awareness, and behaviors, they should leverage students' prior knowledge and experiences (Adams, 2016) regarding social justice topics (see discussion in chapter 1). This principle is important for a few reasons. First, students bring their prior knowledge and experiences into workshops and structured conversations whether or not educators bring this knowledge and experience to the surface. Second, leveraging students' knowledge and experience makes the content more personal and relevant to encourage active student participation. Third, using students' knowledge and experience respects students as coeducators in their learning, thus ensuring the social justice education process mirrors its egalitarian goals.

Educators can address this principle in multiple ways when developing workshops and structured conversations. Educators can select activities where students reflect on their lives. Discussion questions can invite students to draw connections between their lives and the educational content. Further, educators can use activities to create shared experiences among students that replicate social dynamics for students to process relative to their lived experiences. When educators facilitate educational experiences, they can also be mindful of how students participate and invite them to share more deeply, or to call attention to dynamics unfolding in the space (Adams, 2016). Overall, using students' existing and emerging knowledge and experiences advances the goals of social justice education through an intentional process.

A privilege walk is a great way for students to use knowledge and experience. The activity involves educators making statements to which students respond based on the content of their lives. If educators want to further tailor the activity to their students, they can curate a list of statements that are particularly relevant and meaningful to students who are likely to participate. Another way to use a privilege walk to address this principle is for the educator to invite students to discuss which statements from their peers they found familiar and which statements the found surprising.

Principle 3: Help Students Understand Their Multiple Positions Within Systems of Inequality

Social justice education necessarily focuses on systems of inequality in order to envision and create a socially just society. However, students have prior knowledge and experiences that provide real examples of systemic inequality. Therefore, any social justice education experience is incomplete without engaging students and their various life experiences as subjects of learning. This principle requires educators to not only create space for all students to reflect on their experiences but also *invite* students to share their knowledge and experiences as a process where students can specifically examine their roles as actors with specific social identities within inequitable social systems (Adams, 2016). It is important to consider how educators invite students into this process that, in essence, asks students from underrepresented groups to relive marginalizing and traumatic experiences that can be very harmful. By extending an *invitation* rather than an expectation for students to share aloud their personal experiences, educators make clear to students that they have a choice and do not need to carry the burden to educate others. The choice to educate others by sharing their personal experiences is a courageous act. Educators should treat it as such.

Because students have multiple and intersecting social identities, educators should help students think about systems of inequality with respect to their overall positionality (Adams, 2016). This includes exploring both students' privileged and oppressed social identities so they see how they simultaneously experience both sides of inequality that can further their understanding. At a basic level, this requires educators to consider activities that encourage students to examine themselves in relationship to the content areas identified as priorities for the educational experience.

Using the learning outcome example "students will define concepts of *race* and *racism*," educators should do more than lecture to students about these concepts. Further, educators should avoid telling students how they experience race and racism as monolithic truths. Instead, educators should invite students to make sense of the content through the lens of their lived experiences to give the content greater context and meaning. Teaching students about racism through lecture is vastly different from teaching students about racism using their lives as material worth examining. This approach allows students to consider how they experience privilege or oppression and apply these concepts to their lives as they reevaluate their positionality.

A privilege walk satisfies this principle for some, but not all, students who complete this activity. Some statements may help students deepen their understanding of privilege and oppression at a structural level. One one hand, students with privileged social identities associated with the statements read during the activity will likely become more aware of how much privilege they have and the ways in which it permeates their lives. On the other hand, students with oppressed social identities associated with the statements read during the activity are likely already well aware of their positionality. To remedy this situation, the activity might include statements across multiple social identities so that all students can identify the ways they experience privilege and oppression across multiple social identities. Another solution might be to include a discussion activity with questions that explicitly ask students to reflect on how their participation in the activity might look differently with other social identities they hold.

Principle 4: Engage Emotional and Cognitive Aspects of Learning

As students examine systems of inequality through their prior knowledge and various experiences linked to their positionality, they will negotiate both thoughts and *feelings* that influence how they develop knowledge, awareness, and behaviors (Adams, 2016). Beverly Tatum (1994) describes how students can experience a wide range of emotions ranging from excitement to anger when exposed to social justice content. As Bobbie Harro (2013) explains in her cycle of socialization framework, this emotional reaction is sensible because emotions are central to the ideas people hold about people similar to and different from ourselves. If students currently believe that the world is socially just, then they may believe that they deserve whatever they have personally experienced in life. However, when students learn the world is not currently socially just, it can create dissonance with their feelings about the world, others, and themselves. Tim Wise and Kim A. Case (2013) specifically highlight how students from privileged groups commonly feel guilt and shame when learning about their privilege and how they benefit personally from the oppression of others. Similarly, Rita Hardiman and Bailey W. Jackson (1997) describe how students from oppressed groups negotiate feelings of frustration and anger as

they become skilled at identifying the multitude of ways oppression shapes their lives.

Because thoughts and feelings are connected, educators who engage students emotionally and cognitively can use both paths to further students' development (Adams, 2016). Educators who purposefully solicit and engage student emotions can leverage them to advance learning (Goodman, 2011; Watt, 2015). Further, engaging students in emotional work can help them work past shame or guilt and shift to embracing behaviors that contribute to social change (Hardiman, Jackson & Griffin, 2013; Matias, 2016). While some educators may not have patience for engaging students' emotions, emotional development is a critical component in social justice education. Overall, engaging students' emotions in social justice education is both useful and important to ensure social justice education is working toward its goals while humanizing students during the educational process.

Using the previous example learning outcome "students will define concepts of *race* and *racism*," educators can engage students' thoughts and feelings about race and racism. Educators can ask students how they understand race and racism, but they can also ask how race and racism make them feel. Educators can explore where those feelings come from to deepen students' exploration about systems of inequality to make their learning personal. Personalizing learning using students' emotions can help them reconsider content or realities they may originally believe do not affect them.

A privilege walk activity nicely satisfies this principle. When students listen to the statements read aloud, each statement confronts them with examples of privilege or oppression. Additionally, when students are asked to step forward or backward based on each statement, they likely will have an emotional reaction when identifying with a statement, physically taking a step in either direction, and witnessing how many peers do or do not move with them in that moment. It is common to see students wrestle with their emotional responses in the form of how large or small of a step they take as they discern the relevance of each statement and how much attention they wish to draw (or avoid) when moving during the activity. However, adding a discussion activity with questions that explicitly ask students to reflect on the statements and share how they felt when asked to move in response to a statement are powerful ways to further advance students' cognitive and emotional learning.

Principle 5: Establish a Welcoming and Inclusive Environment

Educators must establish a welcoming and inclusive learning environment (Adams, 2016) to actualize the previous four principles. Without a welcoming and inclusive environment, students may be less likely to surface their prior knowledge and experience; examine their positionality related to systems of inequality; and channel their emotions in ways that are educationally productive to the development of knowledge, awareness, and behaviors. Overall, this principle is critical to the success of any social justice education experience.

Educators can establish a welcoming and inclusive environment through the establishment of shared guidelines for interactions during the workshop or structured conversation. Guidelines are an important tool for educators to set expectations for participation and explicitly address how the learning community will engage power dynamics during the experience (Adams, 2016). Further, guidelines signal to students that the quality of their participation matters. This signaling is particularly important for educators to build trust with students from oppressed groups, letting them know that the educator will address problematic comments or behaviors. Sometimes educators might forgo guidelines due to time constraints or because they find them unnecessary given the learning outcomes. However, doing so misses a strategic opportunity to ensure that educators maintain a socially just process in the space.

There are two basic approaches to establishing guidelines. First, educators can create time at the start of the experience to solicit suggestions from students to create guidelines "from the ground up." If educators have time to go this route, students may feel greater investment in adhering to the guidelines because they coauthored them. Second, educators can provide predetermined guidelines and solicit questions or alterations from the students. The benefit of this approach allows educators to ensure specific guidelines are present that they feel capable of maintaining while still providing space for students to cosign them for the experience.

Once guidelines are established, educators must maintain them through active facilitation during the workshop or structured conversation. Maintaining these guidelines requires educators to both model the behavior themselves (which we will discuss more in chapter 5) and actively monitor how students participate and address speech or behaviors that violate the guidelines. However, doing so provides additional opportunities to use students' experiences, thoughts, and feelings during the workshop or structured conversation as learning tools, aligning with the second and fourth principles previously discussed. More about active facilitation strategies useful to maintain inclusive spaces will be discussed in chapter 5.

A privilege walk alone does not satisfy this principle. On the contrary, a privilege walk is a risky activity because it publicly displays students' experiences with privilege and oppression in ways that may make them feel uncomfortable or vulnerable. Therefore, educators should carefully consider a few things before facilitating a privilege walk activity with students. First, establishing community guidelines among students can help create an environment of respect and mutual understanding. Relatedly, the educator must maintain and enforce these community guidelines to cultivate trust among students so that they can be vulnerable or uncomfortable in the educational environment. Second, educators should intentionally time a privilege walk to occur after enough time has passed for the educator to feel assured that students will respectfully engage one another during the activity. Third, the instructions for the privilege walk activity might include a preface that students complete the activity in silence to respect the ways in which different students experience the activity. All of these efforts can help create a space for a privilege walk to be successful.

Selecting Activities

There are multiple ways for educators to satisfy all five principles for social justice education when developing a workshop or structured conversation. Because educators should address these principles through the cumulative experience instead of through each single activity, educators can be creative when selecting activities to support their intended learning outcomes. While multiple hard-copy and digital resources exist with potential activities to implement social justice education, we identify eight activity categories for educators to consider when designing an educational experience.

As previously stated, *guidelines for conversation* is an activity that provides time for students to create or review shared agreements for how to participate in the learning experience. Normally, this activity involves intentional time given near the beginning of the educational experience with the explicit goal of creating a welcoming and inclusive learning environment. Educators can develop guidelines in real time with the students or prepare them in advance. Educators using either format can involve students to discuss and clarify expectations and to commit to each guideline. Guidelines are most effective when they are present in the space, either on a handout or written somewhere where all can see and refer to them during the experience. Depending on the size of the group, level of community among the students, and time allowed for the educational experience, establishing guidelines for conversation may take as few as 5 minutes or as long as 30 minutes.

Many social justice education experiences require educators to present some level of content to their students. However, *lectures* are activities where the educator presents factual information to the students in an intentional, organized manner, such as using handouts or a presentation. Educators using lectures often seek to ensure common knowledge, such as definitions, facts, or events that students know. While lecture is most often associated with traditional teaching methods where educators talk and students listen in order to learn, some level of lecture may be useful for educators to establish basic content that students will build on during the educational experience.

Lectures can be long, such as explaining the history of oppression within the United States, or brief, such as defining core terms and explaining their significance. In workshops and structured conversations, educators are more likely to engage in mini lectures to deliver information that provides a conceptual framework for the focus of student learning. When time is limited, it is important that educators provide enough information to students so that they can engage these concepts and facts without taking time away from the activities that come next. Mini lectures are also advantageous because they prevent students from passively participating for an extended period of time that may entice them to feel like the educational experience is just another academic class lecture.

In addition to guidelines and lectures, educators can have students complete three different types of task-based activities. *Symbolic activities* are activities in which students complete a task where they indirectly engage core concepts or ideas central to social justice through symbolic displacement. Educators can use many icebreaker or energizer activities as symbolic activities. For example, consider the common icebreaker where an educator asks students to form a line based on where they are from without talking. In this activity, students often begin by attempting to establish who is at the front and end of the line based on who is from each coast of the United States. However, students from the middle of the country, as well as students from other countries, tend to struggle to place themselves. Educators can use this activity to symbolize experiences of feeling silenced when talking about their origins and assumptions about what places are perceived to be most valuable. Such activities are typically short, lasting between 5 minutes and 15 minutes. Symbolic activities engage content through displacement, which can be helpful to expose students to large or challenging ideas they might not directly engage otherwise.

Unlike symbolic activities where there is an indirect relationship between the activity and content area, *simulation activities* have students directly engage social justice issues. Simulation activities are activities where students complete a task that replicates social dynamics or experiences useful for exploring how these processes occur or the impact of these processes on themselves or others. One common example described earlier is a privilege walk, where an educator reads various statements and students step forward or backward based on the relevance of the statement to themselves, resulting in students positioning themselves across the room and spatially recreating social stratification. Simulation activities vary widely in duration and are relatively more risky than symbolic activities. Further, simulation activities run the risk of recreating oppressive dynamics that disproportionately teach privileged students at the expense of oppressed students. Simulation activities can be very effective; however, educators should be aware that these activities require trust among students and with the educator before they fully engage in the activity.

When educators ask students to purposefully reflect on their lives, they are facilitating an *introspective activity*. Introspective activities are activities where students complete a task on their own that draws on their personal lived experiences. The primary purpose of introspective activities is to surface students' experiences for intentional exploration relative to taught content. These activities can be tightly structured using premade handouts, or loosely structured asking students to react to a prompt on a sheet of paper. An activity where students identify their social identities and associated values or beliefs would be one example of an introspective activity, because it requires students to intentionally think about their values or beliefs in relationship to their social identities. Because students complete introspective activities individually based on their personal experiences, they may find it easier or harder depending on how much time they have previously spent thinking about their lives in the way the educator frames the discussion.

Lastly, educators can choose discussion-based activities that do not involve completing a task. Discussion-based activities are activities that ask students to generate and share content relative to formulated discussion questions. Whereas task-based activities require attention to completing an objective, discussion-based activities require attention to the students' reactions to these questions. Educators should follow task-based activities with a discussion-based activity to help students make meaning of the task. However, educators may also choose to implement discussion-based activities on their own. Three different variations of discussion-based activities exist depending on the number of students participating in a discussion at any given moment.

Discussion pairs involve two students talking with one another. Discussion pairs are useful to increase the amount of time students have when sharing their reactions to discussion questions. Further, the small size of discussion pairs may be more comfortable for students who are shy or less likely to participate in conversation with larger numbers of students. Discussion questions asking for personal reactions can be most successful in this intimate setting. Lastly, discussion pairs help students practice talking and listening to one person at a time, which can be beneficial when developing interpersonal communication behaviors.

Small group discussions involve three to six students talking with one another. Like discussion pairs, small group discussions allow students to share their reactions to questions in a relatively more intimate setting than a large group. However, having more than two people in a group allows students a greater chance that someone else will connect to their reaction to

the discussion questions. Further, educators can form small groups for discussion based on student characteristics or similar reactions to a discussion question that will support students in simultaneously feeling affirmed and expanding their perspectives. A distinctive benefit for small group discussion is that it provides students an opportunity to practice interpersonal communication behaviors in a group format, which may be a more realistic social setting.

When educators ask students to form pairs or small groups for discussion, there are a few ways they might facilitate this process. If the discussions are less dependent on the social identities of the students, or are relatively low risk, educators might ask students to find a partner or form a group based on proximity ("Partner with someone/the people sitting next to you") to expedite the process. Similarly, educators could ask students to form pairs or small groups based on familiarity ("Find someone you do not know to be your partner"). However, if the discussion questions are dependent on students' social identities, or are relatively higher risk, educators might ask students to form groups in a more particular way. If educators are concerned about students forming groups with their friends or peers with some shared affinity, it is important to consider if these relationships would help or hinder students' ability to engage in the discussion. In some cases, friendship and familiarity may entice students to get off topic. However, there may be times when students pairing up with peers with whom they are familiar is helpful to go deeper in their discussions. Therefore, educators should carefully consider which process for forming pairs or small groups is most useful to advance student learning.

Large group discussions involve groups as large as the entire learning community talking with one another. While large groups do not readily lend themselves to personal sharing, the size makes it highly probable that students will generate varied reactions useful for students to hear and further explore. Additionally, educators might purposefully pose discussion questions that are particularly challenging in large groups so that the entire learning community can collaboratively seek answers. In large group discussions, the educator plays an active role to solicit student participation and build on students' discussion question reactions to highlight important learning takeaways.

When implementing discussion-based activities after task-based activities, discussion questions should resemble an hourglass. Discussion questions should begin by soliciting students' broad reactions, shift to more specific reactions, and then apply these reactions to their broader lives. While there is no magic formula to determine how many discussion questions to prepare in advance, one suggestion is to prepare one or two questions per 5 minutes of discussion time. A useful discussion question template might include some variation of the following questions, depending on the complexity of the task-based activity and the intended learning outcomes:

- What was your experience of the activity?
- What contributed to your reactions to the activity?
- How might the activity feel familiar to your lived experiences?
- What examples from the activity paralleled what we see in society today?
- What could be learned from this activity to help us promote social justice?

Making These Principles Real

After years of trying a variety of methods, I (Roger) have arrived at a pretty specific formula. I have a set of general "ground rules" for each experience that emphasizes a couple of key points: This will be a space for us to share authentically; we are cocreators of this shared experience; and we honor and recognize how each of us shows up emotionally, intellectually, in our social identities, and as a community in this space. I then ask students to collectively create guidelines that we can all adhere to, which maximizes the learning and the chance to build community with one another. This process is an opportunity to see how students engage in the shared process of "setting up the rules" and to gauge their investment in the process.

As we move into the workshop, I make sure to include the most up-to-date and well-referenced data related to the issues we are addressing. This includes providing the definitions of terms, an overview of core concepts, and the historical context of how we arrived where we are today on these issues. I also ask students to make connections from the data to their own experiences and invite them to share how they feel about these connections.

It is generally after students share their perspectives or feelings about the issues when I introduce an interactive simulation or introspective activity designed to personalize

the content for the students. Prior to the activity, I make sure to offer specific guidelines and permission for students to step away if the activity is "hitting too close to home" for them. At the conclusion of the activity, I make time for us to debrief using a discussion-based activity and share the impact of the experience personally, on our community, and for society at large.

I conclude by asking students questions such as the following: What are some key takeaways you learned? What uncertainties did you grapple with? What more do you want to learn? I also emphasize that if they leave with more questions than answers, then they are in a very good place of opportunity to enhance their learning and their growth on these issues.

I (Scott) find myself using a similar "activity formula" for most social justice workshops I design and facilitate to ensure I address all five principles. My activity formula traditionally starts with predetermined guidelines for conversation that I distribute to students and ask them to read aloud. Having students read the guidelines aloud provides students a chance to ask questions and literally give voice to each guideline. My process also serves as a chance for me to observe student dynamics as I gauge how students react to the guidelines and to one another. Next, I provide a mini lecture on core concepts relevant to the workshop. I always begin by naming terms and asking students to both define them and share how they came to understand the concept. Afterward, I provide working definitions for each term and explain that these definitions come from scholarship on this topic. This process allows me to tap into students' prior knowledge and experience while also enhancing their knowledge development.

Having laid a foundation through guidelines and core concepts, I shift to either a symbolic, simulation, or introspective activity, depending on the established learning outcomes, my knowledge about the students and their learning environment, and how much time is available. These task-based activities create a shared experience among students, directly tap into their prior experiences, or both. I follow the activity with either a discussion pair or small group discussion followed by a large group discussion. During discussion pairs or small groups, I ask students to reflect on their reactions to the task-based activity and the various thoughts and feelings that arose during the process. During the large group discussion, I invite students to make connections between the task-based activity and their social identity experiences within the context of systems of inequality. Throughout the discussion, I make connections across students' responses and highlight the relationship between students' emotional and cognitive reactions. I end the discussion with group brainstorming about lessons we have learned to advance social justice. After the discussion, I conclude the workshop with key takeaways to make explicit the knowledge, awareness, and behaviors developed during the experience. To ensure sufficient time for discussion, I attempt to maintain a 1:3-minute activity to discussion ratio because the debrief is where the most learning occurs. This "activity template" is flexible to accommodate shorter workshops and can be expanded to include multiple task-based activities followed by discussion-based activities for longer workshops.

Before finalizing a social justice education workshop or structured conversation, identify how these five principles for social justice education are satisfied related to the activities that will occur. Consider the following questions:

- In what ways are you addressing each principle in the design of the experience?
- What activities would be useful to implement to address multiple principles?

Western College

Creating a 45-minute workshop may feel daunting, but it is achievable because there are only two learning outcomes. Because these workshops occur in the residence halls with residential students, the educator can leverage existing floor agreements created by and for these students. The workshop could begin by reminding students about the guidelines and possibly have them written on flipchart paper and posted in the lounge where the workshop might occur. Additionally, resident advisers could choose to time these workshops to occur after students have had some time to get to know one another and develop trust and rapport during hall social events. The workshop could then shift to a brief, interactive mini lecture that invites students to offer definitions of key terms related to sex and gender. The educator can affirm accurate definitions and clarify those terms for which students are less familiar. This activity simultaneously addresses engaging students' prior knowledge and experience while also addressing the cognitive aspect of learning.

With some foundational knowledge established, the educator could shift to a brief discussion pair activity where students think about how they express their gender and ways they do so that may and may not align with what others expect. This activity would allow students to connect the cognitive to the emotional aspects of learning while further leveraging their lived experiences and exploring their positionality. Afterward, the educator could have a brief large group discussion with a single question asking students to talk about how it felt when people had different expectations of their gender expression. This recognition could be used to pivot to a final activity focused on respectful communication strategies. The educator could present specific strategies to students through another mini lecture while also incorporating students' experiences to highlight how these strategies help prevent students from making assumptions that lead to problematic interactions. This final activity would ensure that students develop behaviors that build on their knowledge and awareness cultivated in the earlier parts of the workshop. The workshop could conclude with a reminder that the proposed communication strategies support whatever floor agreements already exist that are associated with respecting others.

This proposed format for the workshop collectively satisfies all five principles. Using the existing floor agreements and invoking them as guidelines for conversation during the workshop contributes to the fifth principle. The mini lecture contributes to the first and second principles by explicitly cultivating students' knowledge while leveraging their prior knowledge about core concepts. The discussion-based activities contribute to the first, second, and third principles by developing students' awareness of sex and gender, practicing reflection and discussion regarding these topics, and explicitly examining how their gender performance is situated within systems of inequality based on societal expectations. Further, the sequencing of the task- and discussion-based activities collectively address the fourth principle.

Southeastern University

To satisfy all five learning outcomes listed in chapter 3 for the first part of the four-part racial dialogue series, the following outline may be implemented. The educator could begin with introductions where students would be invited to introduce themselves, including their name, their racial identity, why they decided to participate in the racial dialogue series, and what they hope to gain from the experience. Next, students would be invited to cocreate guidelines for conversation for the duration of the dialogue series. These community-generated guidelines would be written on paper and displayed during each dialogue for all students to see. After establishing this foundation for participation, the educator could shift to a mini lecture about race, privilege, oppression, and racism. The educator could invite students to define each term and share why it is relevant for this racial dialogue series. The educator could conclude the lecture portion by sharing working definitions on large sheets of paper to be displayed during each dialogue. Further, if the group decides to modify or add to these definitions during the course of the dialogues, these changes can be made on the paper for all to see. Having the definitions present during the dialogues both reinforce the definitions and invite students to constantly revisit and modify them as they learn together. The mini lecture would end with a brief discussion about intergroup dialogue skills, specifically describing the skills of listening and suspending judgement so that students could practice these skills during the experience.

Because the first dialogue focuses on exploring the impact of racial privilege and oppression and developing reflection and dialogue skills, the next activity would be an introspection activity where students map out their racial timeline, including when they first became aware of race, their racial identity, and significant racial experiences. Students would complete this activity on their own and then shift into discussion pairs to share their timelines and their reactions to the activity. Further, students would be asked to be mindful of the intergroup dialogue skills discussed and to be aware of how it felt to practice these skills in their pairs. Then, the students would transition into a large group discussion where they would talk about what they noticed in their pairs, focusing on differences between the experiences of privileged and oppressed groups and how those differences made them feel. The discussion would shift to reflecting on how racial identities influence their experiences of privilege and oppression and end with some reflection on how it felt to practice listening and suspending judgement during the discussion pairs. Before the dialogue would end, students would review the learning from the dialogue and be invited to pay attention to race, including when they do or do not notice race in their interactions.

This proposed format for the first dialogue collectively satisfies all five principles. Introductions and guidelines for conversation contribute to the fifth principle. The lecture and introspection activity contribute to the first, second, and third principles because they leverage their prior knowledge in defining the concepts and completing the timeline activity. Further, the timeline activity explicitly invites students to consider and become aware of their racialized experiences. The discussion contributes to the first, second, third, and fourth principles because the questions leverage personal experiences to solicit cognitive and emotional reactions that examine systems of racism through their lives.

Handout 4.1
Reflecting on Pedagogical Considerations and Activities
(Building an Outline)

1. List your learning outcomes.

a.

b.

c.

2. Create an outline for your workshop or structured conversation that identifies specific activities, approximate time durations, and specific discussion questions for discussion-based activities.

a.

b.

c.

d.

e.

f.

Five principles

#1: Facilitate the development of knowledge, awareness, and behaviors

#2: Utilize students' knowledge and experiences

#3: Help students understand their positionality within systems of inequality

#4: Engage emotional and cognitive aspects of learning

#5: Establish a welcoming and inclusive environment

3. State which activities address both (a) the learning outcomes on the left and (b) the principles on the right. Modify your outline until it addresses all of your learning outcomes and principles for social justice education.

CHAPTER 5

Facilitation

"We can't teach what we don't know, and we can't lead where we won't go."

—Malcolm X

Facilitation refers to the processes managed and strategies employed when engaging students in learning (Bell, Goodman, & Ouellett, 2016). Additionally, facilitation requires educators to simultaneously use students' social identities and related prior knowledge to generate content and navigate the intrapersonal, interpersonal, and group dynamics that arise from examining their students' lives. Therefore, social justice educators must be prepared to both achieve these goals and model the learning expected of students in the facilitation process. The Malcolm X quote that opens this chapter is a helpful reminder that social justice educators must intentionally prepare themselves with respect to both the content taught and processes managed during the facilitation practice.

Facilitating social justice education workshops and structured conversations is an art and a science. The science of facilitation derives from specific knowledge, awareness, and skills germane to engaging students in their learning. The art of facilitation acknowledges that the ways in which educators perform as facilitators are shaped by who they are, including their social identities, lived experiences, dispositions, and even their sense of humor. A facilitator may be very skilled yet come across as inauthentic if they fail to embrace who they are. Conversely, a facilitator also may be authentic yet unable to perform their role. It is the combination of both the science and artistry that make an educational experience seem "good." This chapter provides an overview of facilitation basics informed by the scholarship of Bell, Goodman, and Ouellett (2016),

Bell, Goodman, and Varghese (2016), and Wah (2004) to provide strategies (the science) and reflective self-work (the art) to help educators bring both together to inform their practice. Because this chapter's primary focus is on the educator instead of the curriculum, we will forgo the running examples applied to Western College and Southeastern University.

Self-Work

Preparing for facilitation always begins with self-reflection because the educator is their own most powerful facilitation tool. Educators bring insights or challenges into the educational experience depending on their level of self-awareness and related topic knowledge. Therefore, educators should engage in self-reflection as an ongoing practice in their lives and intentionally practice self-reflection prior to every educational experience they facilitate. In addition to reflecting on their social identities (as previously discussed in chapter 1), educators should cultivate awareness and knowledge about the areas that influence facilitation through the lens of their personal and social identities: interpersonal style, comfort levels, and how they personally relate to the content and students.

First, educators should reflect on their *interpersonal style* as a facilitator. Reflecting on their interpersonal style includes how they enter into an educational community, how formal or informal they act, their communication preferences and expectations (e.g., providing eye contact, expected verbal participation from students), and how they engage in humor to connect to others (Bell, Goodman, & Varghese, 2016). For example, some educators might desire a formal introduction using their academic or professional titles as an entry point and prefer an "orderly" experience where students raise hands and are called on to speak. Other educators may be informal and introduce themselves using their first name and invite students to speak out without calling on them. When considering our interpersonal style, it is important for the educator to be authentically themselves to avoid trying to be someone they are not. Further, it is critical for educators to consider their interpersonal style through the lens of their social identities to become aware of how their style may influence the type of environment they create and to which student communities they are catering given their approach.

My (Scott) facilitation style is fairly informal. I introduce myself using my first name and prefer when students manage their own participation. However, when multiple students want to speak, or when I want to steer the conversation down a certain path, I shift to calling on students and assigning numbers so that students know when they'll be able to share. I am more traditional in my communication expectations of students and assume eye contact and verbal participation to be indicators of engagement. When students are silent, I make a point to ask what their silence means to prevent myself from making assumptions. However, I always try to check in with students about how they are feeling or what they need to ensure my communication preferences are not skewing my interpretation of the experience.

My (Roger) communication style is one that is very formal in tone, yet often informal in delivery. I introduce myself, share my preferred gender pronouns, and invite students to engage fully but in their own ways. I tell students, "If you are a person who likes to share a lot, there will be opportunities for you to do so. But, this is also an opportunity to work on being inclusive." It is here that I offer the idea of oversharing and how one person dominating the conversation can shut other people down. I also address folks who might be less willing to share. I might say, "For those of you who are more of a listener than a sharer, I do not want you to feel pressure to share, especially deeply personal thoughts, feelings, and experiences, until you are ready. It is absolutely possible for you to engage the material while not sharing much. However, I would invite you to stretch yourself, go against your tendencies, and share your thoughts and perspectives. Doing so could truly enhance the learning for everyone."

Second, educators should also reflect on their *comfort levels* related to silence and emotion. Comfort with silence refers to how one feels when no one is speaking (Bell, Goodman, & Ouellett, 2016). While some educators are comfortable in silence and recognize students need quiet space to think, other educators may feel nervous and assume silence means students are disengaged or uncomfortable. For some, comfort with silence relates to their personal needs when thinking and speaking. Comfort with emotion refers to how one feels when others experience and express their emotions verbally or nonverbally (Bell, Goodman, Varghese, 2016). Some educators may believe that education ought to be factual and objective, and therefore they avoid the realm of emotion. Other educators may feel extremely comfortable with emotion and lean into feelings and emotional reactions during the entire experience. Because the content of social justice education involves concepts tethered to how educators feel about others and themselves, emotion will be present in every experience. Further, when learning about realities and experiences linked to privilege and oppression, individuals may feel an array of emotions, including anger, shame, and hopelessness (Matias, 2016; Wise & Case, 2013).

As I (Roger) mentioned earlier, I feel the need to give permission for students to engage in their own ways. I do this to honor and recognize the role emotion is playing in the experience for each student. I want students to show up authentically, and this means welcoming emotional responses. In instances of lengthy silence, I am patient in allowing the silence to linger and bring about a potentially deep response. In my experience, silence allows precious time for courage and confidence to build in someone who may hesitate or lack confidence, and silence may be just the key factor to encourage some to respond and engage more intentionally.

During facilitation, I (Scott) am extremely comfortable with emotion, frequently comment on emotional shifts in the space, and express gratitude when students express emotion. Similarly, when I pose questions about emotions and students instead provide their thoughts, I redirect them by saying, "I hear you sharing what you think, but I did not hear you express what you feel." However, I constantly work to become more comfortable with silence and need to count to 10 in my head to ensure that I do not rush through moments students need to process information or formulate their responses.

Third, educators should reflect on how they personally *relate to the content and students*. The first part of this reflection involves considering their personal assumptions and biases (Bell, Goodman, & Varghese, 2016). The question is not *if* educators have biases but *what* those biases are and how they manifest themselves. Educators who are unaware of their biases are likely to make assumptions that mischaracterize the content or marginalize students. For example, imagine that an educator is facilitating a workshop related to immigration and race yet is unaware of a bias they hold against undocumented immigrants. If a student makes a comment about "illegals," their bias may prevent them from noticing the student's dehumanizing comment. If the educator did not notice it or challenge it, it could be harmful to students and the educational environment. The second part of this reflection involves considering their triggers (Bell, Goodman, & Varghese, 2016; Obear, 2007). Triggers refer to comments or actions that elicit unconscious emotional responses within a person. Like emotions, triggers are neither good nor bad in themselves; however, the ways educators respond to their triggers can be productive or unproductive to facilitate student learning (Obear, 2007). Educators may be productive when triggered if they are aware of their trigger, able to identify it, and incorporate it as part of the learning experience for students. If educators react to their triggers by pulling themselves away from the educational experience, or if the triggers reduce the educators' capacity to advance the curriculum and fully engage their students, they may be unproductive. Because triggers are often connected to people's experiences informed by their social identities, educators' awareness of their social identities is central to their ability to navigate triggering events and seek support from a cofacilitator during the experience.

When I (Scott) reflect on my biases, assumptions, and triggers, I recognize that I have multiple that manifest themselves differently depending on the content. I hold a biased assumption that White, cisgender male students will be difficult, so when I enter a space I actively make note of those students and remind myself that I do not know their story but will find out soon. Because I am able-bodied and can easily forget about the needs of students with disabilities, I tend to assume that most students are also able-bodied and therefore I speak quickly, prepare presentations that use small fonts and bright colors, and favor activities that require movement. One of my biggest triggers involves jokes or comments that normalize gender-based violence, such as domestic violence. This trigger stems from my personal experience working in a sexual assault prevention office and my relationships with many individuals who have survived these experiences themselves. Specifically, when students use phrases such as "wife beater" to describe an undershirt (the real name being an A-line t-shirt) I might aggressively correct the student's comment if I do not take a moment to recognize my emotional reaction first before responding.

I (Roger) share many of the same assumptions as Scott in regard to individuals from traditionally majority groups that have held power over other groups. I am regularly checking my assumptions by reminding myself of "the danger of a single story" (Adichie, 2009). I also have a number of triggers, most especially in my personal health history. When I hear students sharing the suffering they endured during a health crisis, these stories can sometimes bring me back to my own health scare from 2013. In these moments, I remind myself that I need to facilitate the process and role model for students how to engage while "managing our stuff," a reference to the personal experiences we all have that we can authentically share in this space. I am also potentially triggered by racially and ethnically insensitive comments, which often come from a place of ignorance rather than malice. In these moments, I quickly shift the narrative in my head to understand that in moments like this, it is an opportunity to "awaken" someone and have them come away more informed and more emotionally invested in growing in these matters.

Key Considerations

The act of facilitation requires educators to leverage their knowledge and self-awareness to create and maintain a space conducive for learning. Key considerations for facilitation include student participation, conflict and group dynamics, and the energy of the group (Bell, Goodman, & Ouellett, 2016). These considerations are true for any facilitation experience and mutually influence one another. How well educators moderate the energy of the group will influence group dynamics and individual participation. Similarly, group dynamics that breed unmoderated conflict can prevent students from participating and create an energy in the space that is unsafe for student participation. The nature of social justice education makes these considerations more critical because group dynamics and participation reflect safety or fear linked to the (often unexamined) manifestation of social power students recreate from their social identities. Therefore, these three considerations are essential for educators to effectively facilitate the educational experience.

Additionally, social justice experiences require educators' attention toward additional considerations unique to the process and goals of social justice discussed throughout this book. Beyond moderating participation, educators should ensure multiple voices are present, including those from oppressed groups not present as well as from oneself (Bell, Goodman, & Ouellett, 2016). This task involves an awareness of who is and who is not present and sharing and identifying ways to either cultivate participation from students or insert alternative perspectives. Along the way, educators should encourage students to take risks and practice vulnerability as they (re)examine their assumptions, beliefs, and perspectives about themselves and others (Bell, Goodman, & Ouellett, 2016).

Talking about social identities and personal experiences with social power can be hard for students. One reason for this relates to deeply held misinformation and misconceptions that students adopt. Educators should be aware of common myths and beliefs in order to identify and address them during facilitation (Bell, Goodman, & Ouellett, 2016). Relatedly, educators should surface students' emotions and address them directly (Bell, Goodman, & Ouellett, 2016). If students are fearful of other people further minoritizing them for what they share, educators can validate those concerns to help other students understand them and react with compassion. If students are uncomfortable being emotionally vulnerable, educators can affirm how difficult it can be while also normalizing discomfort as helpful for learning. Because social justice education content is tethered to social identities, the likelihood of students having emotional reactions to these topics is both highly likely and useful to cultivate awareness. Additionally, students' emotions may be connected to their knowledge and beliefs about themselves and others because students' knowledge, beliefs, and emotions reinforce one another. As discussed in chapter 4, this is why Adams (2016) describes the importance of addressing both knowledge and emotions in social justice education.

Sometimes, students might become so overwhelmed with emotion that they disengage, "check out," or become stuck in their feelings that they become immobilized from learning (Bell, Goodman, & Ouellett, 2016). When this happens, educators should be ready to identify these reactions and engage these students and their feelings to move past their paralysis. Not all students are alike in how they behave when feeling overwhelmed. Some commonly observed "signs" include averting eye contact, looking down at their desk or lap, a noticeable change in their participation, or a decline in their energy. What can often help students get "unstuck" is to see what they can do to work toward social change, focusing either on themselves or on the world around them. Identifying next steps for change is useful in these situations and central to any social justice education experience (Bell, Goodman, & Ouellett, 2016). Because social justice is a process and a *goal*, identifying tangible actions or takeaways ensures education leads past enlightenment and into social change.

For example, I (Scott) facilitated a workshop for first-year students about oppression, along with how individuals and institutions maintain oppression in society. I facilitated a simulation activity called "Let Me In" where I told a small group of students to form a circle and keep any other students out. Next, I invited other students to attempt to join the small group of students at the front of the room. After a few minutes of watching students unsuccessfully attempt to join the group (e.g., asking to join while their peers responded with silence, moving toward the group when the group would move away, physically trying to enter the group and other students pushing them back), I facilitated a large group discussion activity to process what happened. When I asked the students who formed the in-group why they acted the way they did, they simply replied, "Well, you told us to act that way." I then highlighted that these students simply followed my instructions even though they had known me for only 5 minutes and further highlighted that the techniques they used to keep students from joining the group they already knew how to do without any instruction. I noticed that many of the students in the workshop became quieter and made less eye contact with me as the large group discussion continued, so I pointed out what I noticed among the group and asked the students to share how they were feeling in that moment. One student shared that they felt bad about how they acted and did not know what else to do or say. It was in the moment that I normalized their feelings and had their attention to begin talking about ways to become more aware of how they maintain oppression in their lives and small actions they could take moving forward.

Skills

Facilitating educational experiences in ways that are mindful of these key considerations requires multiple skills. While some skills may seem self-evident, it is important that educators intentionally remind themselves of these skills to ensure their practice is congruent with the described purpose.

Creating Relationships With Students

Social justice education is highly personal because it examines lived experiences and the ways people benefit or suffer from social inequality. Talking about these experiences produces a range of emotions and reactions educators must engage. Effective facilitation requires educators understand this dynamic and honor the humanity of students by creating relationships. Students are more likely to participate and lean in when they feel their full humanness matters in the experience.

Wah (2004) provides excellent strategies for developing relationships. First, ask for and use a student's name when directly engaging with them. For example, if the educator asks a question to the group and calls on a student, they can consider saying "Hello. What is your name?" before asking, "What would you like to share?" Asking and using students' names both humanizes them and reduces their ability to feel invisible when sharing. Second, consider moving closer to the student who is speaking. Closing the distance between the educator and the student can increase how trusting and candid they are when speaking. Third, when students finish speaking, thank them for contributing. This simple gesture gracefully ends the interaction while opening the door for other students to share. Taken together, these steps are similar to those taken when meeting a stranger at a party: Both people introduce themselves, close the distance between each other to speak, and then conclude with appreciation for one another.

Listening and Observing

An essential part of developing relationships involves seeing and listening to others. It requires educators to be present when they are with students. This involves discipline to avoid being distracted by what they are going to say, how they feel, or other diversions that take attention away from the student. Listening and observing involves paying attention to what students say explicitly and mean implicitly. Listening to what students say is straightforward; however, it does not mean educators hear everything that students say. Hearing students involves both the explicit words they share and the implicit feelings and beliefs that accompany their words. Observing students involves noticing their nonverbal communication. Observations should include their body language (e.g., eye contact, arm position), body positioning (e.g., do they lean toward or away), and their vocalisms (e.g., tone, volume, speech pattern), which provide information about what they may think and feel in the moment. Listening to and observing what is "said," both explicitly and implicitly, requires educators to be fully present or possibly miss key information that could help facilitate the experience.

The concept of TING is particularly helpful for listening and observing. TING is a Chinese character that represents the concept of deep listening. However, this single character consists of six smaller characters that include eyes, ears, mind, heart, unity, and royalty. Taken together, listening with TING means the educator should listen with their ears (listening) and their eyes (observing) along with their mind (what students' mean) and their heart (what students' feel). However, to listen with TING involves listening to students with the same respect and presence the educator would offer someone of royalty with the goal of listening for what brings people together. Listening with TING is helpful because it encapsulates the notion of being fully present when listening and observing what students share explicitly and implicitly. Lastly, it reminds educators that the goal in facilitation is to bring people together for increased understanding and unity.

Responding

Educators also need skills for responding to students *after* they listen and observe what students share. Responses should be directed toward a specific student, idea, or feeling. Making the focus of the response clear can be explicit (e.g., saying "Jake shared a comment that we should take a moment to unpack") or implicit (e.g., moving closer and facing the student who the comment is directed toward). Directing the response is important to ensure students understand the context of the educator's remarks and reduces the chance of misinterpreting the comments as a personal attack.

Educators should be mindful of five different ways to respond and the goals they are trying to accomplish.

Educators might *respond with empathy* in order to connect to students, to humanize what they have shared, or to normalize feelings and ideas. Responding with empathy involves making explicit connections between themselves and what a student shared (e.g., saying "I can appreciate that feeling. I've been there myself."). Other times educators respond in order to move deeper into content. Educators might *respond with questions* when a student shared something that is unclear (e.g., asking "Can you tell me what you mean when you use the word 'oppression' in your story?"). Educators might also paraphrase what a student shared and pose a question to ensure they understood it correctly before exploring their ideas or feelings in greater depth (e.g., asking "How did the experience make you feel in that moment?"). Educators could pose questions to a single student or use a question to pivot from a single student to the large group and invite others into the topic. All questions should be clear and concise to help students better understand the current topic of exploration. Educators could also *respond with information* to provide useful ideas that build on what a student shared. For example, if a student describes a personal experience with *intersectionality* without using that term, educators might use the opportunity to share the term to help all students develop language for their experiences (e.g., saying "Scholars would call that an example of intersectionality. If interested, consider checking out Kimberlé Crenshaw's 1991 article called 'Mapping the Margins.'").

Educators often find themselves needing to respond to something problematic or inaccurate that a student shared. In these moments, educators might *respond with challenge* to indicate their disagreement with what a student shared before examining the topic further. When responding with challenge, it is critical to be clear about the focus of the response (e.g., saying "I need to address an assumption behind what was just said so we can examine if there is truth behind it."). Often responding with challenge focuses on a specific comment or the sentiment behind a comment. Making it clear that the focus is not about the student helps prevent students from feeling attacked or judged, which may inspire other students to shut down or withdraw from participation. Other times, educators might need to *respond with interruption* in order to stop a student from monopolizing time or continuing to say things that may be harmful. Interrupting students is challenging because educators

must be careful to do so without contradicting an environment that invites open participation. When responding with an interruption, educators should be clear about why they are choosing to do so (e.g., saying "There is a lot you just said that I'd like to unpack; I just noticed the room react to what you just said so I'd like to pause your comments so we can bring others into the moment with us."). Educators might consider moving closer to the student and gently placing an arm on their shoulder to maintain the relationship with that student.

Sharing Information

Facilitation requires educators to artfully blend the solicitation of information from students with information shared by the educator. Sharing information is an essential skill to influence reflection; generate new awareness; and stoke cognitive and emotional dissonance for students to notice and explore their ideas, beliefs, and feelings. Sharing information should be timely to move the educational experience forward; however, the purpose of sharing information is not to assert one's expertise or authority (and not jeopardize the environment and relationships they have created). When sharing information, educators should always consider what they should share and how they should use specific information to further student learning. What to share can include facts and experiences. When to share information may occur proactively, such as offering a definition before discussion or reactively when students discuss topics that require terms or ideas to further their exploration. For example, an educator might share their own racial experience to start a conversation about students' racial experiences, or they might find themselves discussing *race*, *ethnicity*, and *nationality* and find it helpful to define these terms to help students' reflections. When sharing information, it is always helpful to accompany the information with its source, whether it is scholarship, research, or an individual's lived experience. While sharing the source does not need to be formal, it helps to establish that the information shared is rooted in fact.

Self-Disclosure

One of the best facilitation tools is the lived experience of the educator. Goodman (1995) discusses how self-disclosure helps provide content for reflection and models how students ought to participate in the workshop or structured conversation. As discussed in chapter 1, the educator is a key contextual influence. Therefore, educators should consider how to use those experiences to further student learning.

Self-disclosure includes sharing personal experiences with students and naming thoughts and feelings during the experience. Sharing these experiences can be a form of sharing information or a way to bring alternative perspectives and realities into the space that is not there. It is particularly helpful when educators self-disclose experiences and challenges with privilege or oppression to help students acknowledge these realities and see ways to navigate them for themselves. Sharing thoughts and feelings is equally as powerful at normalizing them as modeling how to engage them in ways that are productive and not harmful to other students. For example, it may be helpful to name when an educator feels triggered by what a student says and continue to narrate how they process those feelings.

There is a fine line between self-disclosure to advance student learning and sharing things that center oneself in the educational experience. When considering self-disclosure, educators should be mindful of whose needs are being met. While it is always okay to think and feel things during facilitation, self-disclosure is not the same as equal participation. When self-disclosing, be sure to not share in ways that make oneself the center of the experience. It is helpful for educators to invest time before and after a facilitation experience to become aware of their needs and triggers and to avoid centering themselves in the experience.

Soliciting Participation

Cultivating student participation is essential to engaging students' prior knowledge and leveraging their experiences for learning. Soliciting participation focuses on how educators intentionally engage students with the goal of increasing participation. When soliciting participation, educators might pose questions to a specific student, the entire group, or a subcommunity of students. Student subcommunities often include social identity groups; they also include groups based on what educators observe, including "those who have not yet participated" or "students in the back of the room." It is helpful to pose questions as invitations (e.g., asking "I've noticed that Miki has not shared yet—is there something you would be willing to share with us on this topic?") to respect students' agency in the experience while still helping create

space for students who want to participate. The goal is to ensure all students have space to participate if they are willing.

It is equally important to ensure participation is equitable among students. Educators should observe who is, and who is not, participating and respond with questions to call attention to this dynamic (e.g., asking "I'm noticing that only students of color have spoken about racism. Would any White students like to share?"). Calling attention to dynamics related to participation may lead to students wanting to talk because they believe the educator actually notices them. When students feel noticed, it contributes to the relationship development between the educator and the student. Invitations to participate can focus on specific students or students from a specific social identity group depending on what educators observe and want to achieve. Again, the goal is to make space for all students to participate.

Reading the Room

Facilitation requires educators to engage students as a collective group in addition to them as individuals. Educators must use their listening and observation skills to engage the students as a collective unit. This task includes noticing *and* responding to three things: group reactions to individual students, student participation patterns, and energy shifts in the space.

Reading the room requires noticing what happens in the space and using it to facilitate student learning. If there is a change in energy or decline in participation after a particular student speaks, it is essential for educators to notice this event, name it, and invite students to help navigate the experience. For example, educators might ask, "Does anyone feel as if the energy got sucked out of the room just now, and, if so, why might that be?" Similarly, educators might say, "I notice students who have self-identified as White have been silent during our conversation on race. Why is that?" Naming what happened and inviting students to make sense of it allows educators to reengage students and use it as part of the learning experience.

Creating Connections

During a workshop or structured conversation, educators should be prepared to help students make connections among content areas and student experiences. While the connections among concepts may seem self-evident to students, educators should make these connections explicit to ensure students' understanding. Creating connections among student experiences can be more challenging. Educators can use skills for listening, observing, and reading the room to help students connect their experiences to one another based on what is explicitly said (e.g., stating "What Shelby just shared is similar to Tonya's comment earlier") or the feelings expressed (e.g., saying "I can feel the frustration behind your comment Shemar. Does anyone else share Shemar's frustration?").

Educators should also create connections across content areas and student experiences. This task requires a delicate balance between helping students develop language for their experiences while not putting words into their mouths. Naming students' experiences for them takes away their agency and runs the risk of making wrong assumptions that harm educators' abilities to maintain the relationships they have created. Educators can ask questions that help students make these connections themselves (e.g., asking "What connection do you see between what you just shared and our conversation on structural racism?") or use self-disclosure to connect to the content themselves and then invite students to relate to their experience. Both approaches allow educators to make explicit connections without labeling students' experiences for them.

Finding (and Creating) Transitions

Transitions include moving (a) from one activity to the next in the curriculum, (b) among different students who are sharing, (c) from time for student sharing to structured activities, and (d) from the curriculum to addressing a pressing issue (termed *off-roading*). The ability to find or create transitions is essential in partnership with the skills previously discussed. Educators will often listen and observe while also reading the room to identify natural moments for transition. It is ideal to find and leverage natural moments for transition in order to maintain students' interest or increase their energy. For example, educators may notice students with blank expressions, which could be a cue to move onto the next activity or pivot into an energizer. However, educators may also need to create transitions. Educators often create transitions to respond with an interruption or to balance student sharing with the need to move forward in the curriculum. When creating a transition, educators should be careful to do so without feeling abrupt (e.g., saying "Forgive me for interrupting, but there is a lot in what you shared that deserves to be unpacked if that is alright with you.").

A useful approach to navigating transitions involves narrating the transition aloud to students. When educators find a moment for transition, they might acknowledge it as a statement (e.g., saying "It seems like we have robustly answered this question, so let's explore this next one.") or as a question (e.g., asking "The energy feels like it is sagging now; should we move onto the next activity?"). Educators might also provide additional information to help students understand why the transition is happening (e.g., saying "I hate to stop this great conversation, but we have one last activity that I think you all will appreciate."). Narrating transitions is helpful so that students follow the flow of events and understand why everything is happening to stay engaged in the learning experience.

The LARA Method

Bonnie Tinker (2004) developed the LARA method, a specific practice that uses multiple facilitation skills to aid student learning, especially when students say problematic things that require a direct challenge. LARA is an acronym for a multi-step process where educators (a) listen, (b) affirm, (c) respond, and (d) add information. Educators must listen with TING to what students are saying, including what they explicitly say along with any expressed values or feelings. Only after educators listen should they move to the next step of affirmation. Affirmation requires educators to find something to acknowledge as a source of common ground they share with the student. For example, after listening deeply an educator might affirm the importance of a shared value or indicate agreement with part of their statement. However, it is important to note that affirmation is not the same as agreement. The goal of affirmation is to establish commonality and humanize one another in the interaction. Affirmation can be difficult; however, it is the most critical step in the process.

Educators should respond only after they offer some affirmation. In the LARA method, responding involves educators directly expressing what they think (e.g., saying "I disagree with your comment."). A direct response clarifies the stance educators take while also allowing them to be clear when challenging something problematic. Finally, educators conclude by adding information that contributes to the sharing of knowledge and experiences. This can include sharing facts from scholarship or news sources, personal anecdotes to bring the conversation to a real experience, or posing a question to invite others to add information into the exchange.

Consider the following example to make the LARA method clear. Imagine a White student says, "I don't think conversations about White privilege should blame me for the actions of White people who I never knew and who were alive before I was born." The educator uses the LARA method and *listens* for what a student says and what they are feeling. This student does not think people should be blamed for things they did not personally do. Further, they feel upset that they are associated with people they never knew because they both are White. Altogether, they hold a value for fairness that feels violated. Based on listening deeply for these elements, the educator can *affirm* many things the student said, saying, "I appreciate how frustrating it is to be lumped in with other people based on a single social identity. I also appreciate how unfair it can feel to be associated with things you personally did not do." Notice in these affirmation statements the educator affirms the broader ideas and feelings within the students' original statement but that this is not a form of agreement. Next, the educator could *respond* to the immediate comment by stating, "I disagree that conversations about White privilege blame White people for things they did not do because there is a difference between causing privilege and perpetuating privilege." Lastly, the educator could *add information* to make clear the distinction between structural causes of privileges and individual actions that perpetuate privilege, using their own experiences as an example.

The following are questions to ask before facilitating a workshop or structured conversation:

Self-work

- What are your interpersonal style and related expectations of students when facilitating an educational experience?

- How comfortable are you with silence and expression of emotion, and how do you react when these occur?
- What biases, assumptions, and triggers do you hold regarding the content of the experience or the students with whom you will work?

Capacity for key considerations

- What do you expect regarding student participation, and how do you help moderate participation?
- How do you typically react to conflict, and what is your approach to moderating conflict between students?
- How attentive are you to who is present and engaged, and how might you solicit engagement from students?
- How aware are you of common myths and misconceptions regarding social justice content, and how do you tend to react when others share myths or misconceptions?
- How do you personally stay hopeful and present when faced with overwhelming challenges to social justice, and how might you share these strategies with others?

Reflecting on skills

- For each of the following skills, how would you rate your level of competence and confidence?
  - Creating relationships with students
  - Listening and observing
  - Responding
  - Sharing information
  - Self-disclosure
  - Soliciting participating
  - Reading the room
  - Creating connections
  - Finding and creating transitions

Handout 5.1
Reflecting on Facilitation: Self-Work

1. When facilitating, think about each of the following aspects of facilitation and how they are connected to your social identities:

a. Interpersonal style:

b. Comfort with silence:

c. Comfort with emotion:

d. Potential biases:

e. Potential assumptions:

f. Potential triggers:

Reflecting on Facilitation: Skills

2. For each of the following facilitation skills, rate yourself on how competent you are with that skill, how confident you are with that skill, and any notes about things you do well or struggle with related to that skill:

a. Creating relationships with students

Competence	Confidence	Notes

b. Listening and observing

Competence	Confidence	Notes

c. Responding

Competence	Confidence	Notes

d. Sharing information

Competence	Confidence	Notes

e. Self-disclosure

Competence	Confidence	Notes

f. Soliciting participation

Competence	Confidence	Notes

g. Reading the room

Competence	Confidence	Notes

h. Creating connections

Competence	Confidence	Notes

i. Finding (and creating) transitions

Competence	Confidence	Notes

CHAPTER 6

Assessing Student Learning

Imagine that a social justice education workshop or structured conversation has attracted the attention of a university president. The president not only comes to the event but also invites the educator who oversaw the event to their office to share more about their work. After reviewing the curriculum, the president asks for data that shows how effective it was. Does the educator have data to answer their question? What types of data might they present?

- Students' ability to directly demonstrate learning
- Students' self-reported data on the event's effectiveness
- Satisfaction data from the students
- General open-ended comments from the students
- Anecdotal feedback from a few students after the experience

Ideally, they would have direct evidence of students' ability to demonstrate learning linked to the established learning outcomes because this would be the most compelling evidence one could present. The other types of data are not bad; however, they are less effective at answering how effective the educational experience was for students.

While this scenario is unlikely, it forces social justice educators to consider their capacity to measure their effectiveness and use data to drive improvement. As St. Vincent DePaul said, "It is not enough to do good, it must be done well." For social justice educators, this means that only developing and facilitating social justice education experiences is insufficient. Educators must also be able to assess student learning

and use that information to continually improve their impact on students.

What Assessment Is, Is not, and Should Be

It is common to hear practitioners use the terms *assessment* and *evaluation* interchangeably, even though they are distinct. Walvoord (2010) defines *assessment* as "the systematic collection of information about student learning, using the time, knowledge, expertise, and resources available, in order to inform decisions about student learning" (p. 2). Notice how the definition of *assessment* explicitly connects to student learning in both the data collected and how educators use the data to drive improvement. Conversely, *evaluation* could be defined as the systematic collection of information in order to judge the quality or value of a program or experience. In this definition of *evaluation*, the focus is not on student learning but on the quality of the experience itself.

While both assessment and evaluation are processes that collect data to make decisions, they rely on different types of data to make different types of decisions. Assessment collects data related to students' knowledge, awareness, and behaviors they should attain as stated in a learning outcome statement. Assessment uses this data to identify ways to improve instruction to increase student learning. Conversely, evaluation collects a wider range of data that may include student satisfaction, rates of participation, or cost-benefit ratios to determine if an experience is effective. While student learning assessment data can sometimes be used for evaluation purposes, evaluation data cannot be used as evidence of student learning.

The distinction between assessment and evaluation is important because different types of data can be useful for different purposes. Knowing how many students attend an event can be useful to determine how many times to host a workshop or structured conversation. Knowing if students are satisfied with an experience can be useful to increase affinity with an institution. However, while these types of data have their place, it is important to note that they are not the same as the type of data necessary for learning assessment. The only way to assess student learning is to collect data on students' knowledge, awareness, or behaviors linked to an established learning outcome. Educators need this data to determine how effectively their event promotes student learning. Additionally, if they discover the educational experience is not effective, then this data will illuminate ways to enhance the experience to increase student learning in the future. For these reasons, this book focuses solely on assessment.

Furthermore, assessing student learning should be a transparent process. When educators explicitly tell students what they will learn and how they will be assessed, students are more successful in demonstrating learning, and it helps close achievement gaps (Winkelmes et al., 2019). Transparency in assessment includes sharing the learning outcomes with students, telling students how they will be assessed, and informing students how educators will use the assessment data they collect. When students know the learning outcomes for an experience and how educators will assess student learning, they are primed to pay attention in ways that will guide their learning. While some educators might view this as "cheating," it is critical to differentiate between telling students the correct answers on a quiz or prompt versus informing them about the content they will learn and be assessed on in the experience. For example, just because students are told they will learn the definition of *privilege* and be expected to define *privilege* at the end of a workshop does not mean they will be successful. On the contrary, transparency in assessment is a way to set expectations for learning and increase students' chances for success.

Steps for Assessing Student Learning

Assessing student learning is essentially a five-step process similar to a cycle of inquiry:

1. Identify the learning outcome statement.
2. Determine the data to be collected and from whom.
3. Develop necessary tools to collect and analyze data.
4. Collect data.
5. Analyze and use data to improve the educational experience.

Let us discuss each step and how educators can move through the process.

Step 1: Identify the Learning Outcome Statement

At the center of assessment is a learning outcome statement. Therefore, the first step must always be to determine which learning outcomes to assess. If educators have multiple learning outcome statements, they may not be able to assess all of them at the same time due to time constraints. To decide which learning outcomes to assess first, choose those that are foundational to the education experience. For example, educators might start with the "easiest" learning outcomes that they believe students ought to master in order to be successful with the other learning outcomes. Educators who find themselves uninterested in assessing one or more of the learning outcomes may find it helpful to revise the learning outcome statements to ensure they find the statements meaningful (see the discussion about best practices for writing learning outcomes in chapter 3).

Step 2: Determine the Data to be Collected and From Whom

After determining which learning outcome statements to assess, social justice educators need to determine what information they need to collect that will provide evidence of student learning. Do they need information about students' knowledge, awareness, or behaviors? Should students provide this information by identifying the correct answer from a list of options, by providing an answer written in their own words, or by their observable actions in real time? A well-written learning outcome statement will make the type of information needed clear.

Reflecting back on the parts of a learning outcome statement described in chapter 3, the behavior of a learning outcome refers to the specific content that students are expected to learn. When a learning outcome statement clearly describes the behavior, it tells the educators what information they should collect from students and in what format based on the action verb. Consider the following two learning outcome behaviors:

Behavior 1: Identify definitions of *race* and *racism*
Behavior 2: Define *race* and *racism*

The types of data needed for both behaviors include definitions of two concepts—*race* and *racism*. However, the verb used in relationship to each behavior suggests different types of information. Behavior 1 requires information about definitions of *race* and *racism* that students identify from a list of options. However, behavior 2 requires information about these same definitions provided by students in their own words. Even though the content is the same, how educators expect students to demonstrate learning alters the type of information they need to collect based on the level of learning expected. There is a difference between picking the right definition from a list versus coming up with the definition on one's own.

Step 3: Develop Necessary Tools to Collect and Analyze Data

Once the educator has an understanding of what data they need to collect and from whom they will collect it, they can develop tools for data collection and analysis. Depending on the type and format of data they need to collect, multiple tools may be necessary. While numerous options exist, this book discusses tools most commonly used for social justice education workshops and structured conversations. These tools include learning surveys, writing prompts, and rubrics. The following information represents insights from Nilson (2010) and Suskie (2009), along with our professional experience.

Learning surveys, most commonly referred to as tests or quizzes, consist of a series of questions students complete to assess their learning. While learning surveys can include open-response questions, most include multiple-choice questions with predetermined answer choices from which a student selects an answer. Some multiple-choice questions will have a single right answer. Single-answer multiple-choice questions are useful when educators want students to determine the best answer among all possible options. This type of multiple-choice question is relatively

easy for students to complete because they can narrow down the right answer through deduction. Other multiple-choice questions have multiple answers. These questions commonly ask students to "select all that apply" because more than one option may be correct. Multiple-answer questions are harder than single-answer questions because students cannot narrow down choices to find the correct answer. Instead, students must consider each option independently. Single-answer questions may be useful to assess basic content knowledge (e.g., "Select the statement that is true regarding the definition of *privilege*."), while multiple answer questions may be useful to assess content knowledge and behaviors (e.g., "What are the essential components of dialogue? Select all that apply."), as shown in Figure 6.1 and Figure 6.2.

Learning surveys that use multiple-choice questions are the most straightforward measurement tool because educators can use them to both collect *and* analyze data as all possible answers are predetermined in advance to be correct or incorrect. Writing multiple-choice

FIGURE 6.1. Example of a single-answer survey question.

Select the statement that is TRUE regarding the definition of *privilege*:

Option A	Refers to benefits, rights, and access given based on someone's social identities and exists at an individual level only
Option B	Refers to benefits, rights, and access given based on someone's personal accomplishments and exists at an individual and institutional level
Option C	Refers to benefits, rights, and access given based on someone's personal accomplishments and exists at an individual level only
Option D	Refers to benefits, rights, and access given based on someone's social identities and exists at an individual and institutional level

Note. Tharp (2017)

FIGURE 6.2. Example of a multiple-answer survey question.

What are the essential components of dialogue? Select all that apply:

Option A	Active listening
Option B	Advancing your personal agenda
Option C	Using "I" statements
Option D	Finding commonality

questions requires educators to know in advance the data they need to collect in order to write the question as well as to know common misconceptions in order to write incorrect answer options. The use of common misconceptions as wrong answer options is a helpful way to diagnose continued misunderstanding that persists after the education experience ends. Such information is valuable to have when reviewing the results later to determine how to improve the educational experience in the future.

Learning surveys are extremely versatile for a wide range of audiences and conditions. They can be collected in hard copy (e.g., pen and paper) or digital form (e.g., distributed online). Further, they can ask multiple questions or a single question depending on what information the educators need and how much time they have. Therefore, learning surveys are a great option for educators with little time to assess learning at the very end, or after, a learning experience. Educators who worry about students feeling like they are taking a test can be creative when using learning surveys. At the end of the education experience, the educator can post a question on flip-chart paper and ask students to write their answers on a note card. Tech-savvy educators can include a question on a PowerPoint slide and ask students to "text" their answer using student polling software such as Poll Everywhere. Such software collects students' answers live and allows educators to discuss these answers with students to further engage their learning.

It is best to avoid learning survey questions that ask students to report their opinion about their learning. It may be tempting to ask questions such as, "How effective was this learning experience?" or "How much did you learn today?" These questions provide students' perceptions about the educational experience but not evidence of student learning relative to a specific learning outcome. Even if 100% of students indicate the learning experience was highly effective, those results do not indicate students' knowledge, awareness, or behaviors that educators expect them to demonstrate and thus are not useful.

Writing prompts are tools that provide an openedended question for students to answer in their own words without using preselected answer options. Unlike learning surveys that are designed to be quicker to complete, written prompts require more time because students are generating the answers themselves. Writing prompts can vary in length, being

as short as a single sentence or as long as a multiple-paragraph essay. The length of the response depends on how much information the prompt requests from the student. A prompt that asks students to define *racism* in their own words may be a few sentences. However, a prompt that asks students to describe at least two ways they have experienced privilege or oppression in their lives may be a few paragraphs. Writing prompts are quicker to create than surveys because all that needs to be developed is a question to collect data. However, these prompts also require a rubric to analyze the data collected.

Shorter writing prompts are easiest to complete when they involve a few sentences or less. Examples of short writing prompts may include asking students to (a) define *privilege*, (b) name at least one personal identity where they are privileged, or (c) describe how they have benefited from privilege. As evidenced by these examples, short writing prompts can collect a wide range of data about content knowledge and application to lived experiences. Educators can easily incorporate short writing prompts after or at the end of a learning experience. Creative educators might provide a prompt on flip-chart paper for students to complete using a small note card they turn in. Students could turn in their note card before they leave the workshop or structured conversation, or educators could ask students to drop off their note card at a campus location later that week.

Longer writing prompts are also an option for social justice educators to consider. If educators cannot provide students time to complete longer responses during the education experience or cannot reasonably ask students to complete a longer response and submit a week or more after the experience, the likelihood of getting good data, or any data at all, may decline. However, if educators are looking to assess student communities where they do have long-term access, such as resident advisers who are in a year-long position, longer prompts may be a great option.

Educators should also consider creating writing prompts or learning survey questions that use scenarios. Scenario-based questions or prompts present students with information they should use to answer the question. The benefit of proving a scenario in conjunction with either learning survey questions or writing prompts is to provide students the opportunity to demonstrate learning related to a specific context they might not readily experience firsthand. Scenarios could replicate interactions with specific people (e.g., other students) or a specific environment (e.g., the workplace). Asking students to respond to a scenario allows educators to assess student learning that they expect students to apply in one or more situations. For example, a writing prompt may ask students to provide an example of a microaggression. However, a scenario-based writing prompt may ask students to read a scenario and identify the microaggressions that are present in the scenario. Scenario-based questions or prompts allow educators to assess more complex learning outcomes or collect data related to environments they may not be able to replicate or directly observe themselves.

Educators should avoid writing prompts such as "Tell me one thing you learned today." This prompt is useful to provide general insight into what content students believe they learned, but it does not solicit evidence of student learning expected through a learning outcome. There is a difference between students who define *oppression* in their own words versus those who say, "I learned about oppression." It is important to remember that assessing student learning seeks to determine the extent to which learning has occurred, *not* what students believe they learned.

Rubrics are the final common tool used by social justice educators. Rubrics are structured guides used to analyze data that consist of three parts: criteria, rating categories, and descriptions. Criteria refer to the specific aspects of student learning an educator will assess. Rubrics can have multiple criteria or just one criterion. For example, writing prompts asking students to define *oppression* and describe examples of oppression in their lives may require multiple criteria to analyze the quality of their definition and their

examples. However, a writing prompt that asks for a short definition of *oppression* may have only one criterion for the definition's quality.

Rating categories refer to the various ways educators might "grade" the quality of students' responses. Rubrics can have as few as two rating categories (e.g., unsatisfactory, satisfactory) depending on the potential range of responses you anticipate from students. However, most rubrics have three rating categories for student responses that are below expectations, meets expectations, or exceeds expectations. One benefit of using three rating categories is that it allows room for students' responses to be above or below what educators expect them to produce, which can inform future educational experiences.

Lastly, descriptions refer to the quality of the response at each rating level within each criterion. What exactly does a definition of *oppression* that meets expectations look like? How might it look if it exceeds expectations? Descriptors are essential to help educators distinguish various student responses. However, descriptors can be challenging to create because they require educators to have a clear distinction between bad, good, or great responses. To make this clear, consider the example rubric in Table 6.1 used to assess data from a writing prompt that asks students to define *oppression* and describe examples of oppression in their own lives.

In this example rubric, there are two criteria—one for the definition of *oppression* and one for the examples of oppression. Also, there are three rating categories that include below, meets, or exceeds expectations. Lastly, there are six descriptions—one for each rating category relative to both criteria. While this example provides one potential set of descriptors, they can vary

TABLE 6.1. Example of a Rubric on Oppression

	Below Expectations	*Meets Expectations*	*Exceeds Expectations*
Definition of Oppression	Student expresses fewer than two core ideas of oppression in their definition *or* expresses at least one inaccurate idea	Student expresses *at least two* core ideas of oppression in their definition without any inaccurate ideas	Student expresses *three or more* core ideas of oppression in their definition without any inaccurate ideas
Examples of Oppression	Student inaccurately applies oppression to one of their social identities	Student accurately applies oppression to *one* of their social identities	Student accurately applies oppression to *two or more* of their social identities

TABLE 6.2. Example of a Rubric on Dialogue Skills

	Below Expectations	*Meets Expectations*	*Exceeds Expectations*
Active listening	Student uses *neither* appropriate eye contact *nor* encouraging nonverbal behaviors when listening to their peers	Student uses *either* appropriate eye contact *or* encouraging nonverbal behaviors when listening to their peers	Student uses *both* appropriate eye contact *and* encouraging nonverbal behaviors when listening to their peers
Using "I statements"	Student *seldom* uses "I" statements when dialoguing with their peers	Student *occasionally* uses "I" statements when dialoguing with their peers	Student *frequently* uses "I" statements when dialoguing with their peers

widely based on the expectations of the educator and the content taught during the educational experience.

Rubrics are essential for analyzing data collected through writing prompts. Educators can also create a rubric to analyze observed behavior the same way; however, educators would base the criteria on the aspects of behavior they expect students to demonstrate. For example, imagine an educator is facilitating a structured dialogue that teaches students essential behaviors to participate in dialogue. They could create a rubric with separate criteria for each expected behavior that includes active listening and using "I" statements, as illustrated in Table 6.2.

While this book discusses learning surveys, writing prompts, and rubrics as common tools for assessing student learning, many more exist. However, these three tools will help educators assess the majority of student learning outcomes they are most likely to craft for social justice education workshops and structured conversations.

Step 4: Collect Data

Equipped with the tools and knowledge about whom they will assess, educators are ready to collect their data. While collecting data is self-explanatory, it is essential to clarify from whom they will collect data and when this will happen. A well-written learning outcome statement will make this explicit due to the stated audience and condition. In a learning outcome statement, the audience refers to the students that educators expect will demonstrate learning, and the condition refers to the specific experience that students will complete related to their learning. When developing their learning assessment, they should collect data from this same group of students. For example,

if the learning outcome statement focused on students who participated in at least two workshops, then the educator should collect data only from students who meet this criterion. Additionally, the condition will influence when and how data will be collected for the learning assessment. If the condition involves participating in an optional experience, the educator might consider collecting data at the end of the workshop or structured conversation when they have access to these students. However, if the condition involves participating in a certain number of experiences over a period of time, they might need to collect data sometime after the educational experience has ended.

Educators might collect data during, at the end of, or sometime after the educational experience. When educators collect data during the educational experience, it is considered *formative assessment*. One notable benefit of formative assessments is that educators can use the results to modify and adapt the educational experience to meet to students' needs or address content not sufficiently learned before moving forward. For example, educators can use a learning survey on terms and definitions offered in the middle of a workshop to facilitate a conversation about these terms and address lingering misconceptions before moving to the next activity or content domain. However, when educators collect data at the end of, or after, an educational experience, it is considered *summative assessment*. Summative assessments occur at the point in time when educators reasonably expect students to have mastered the learning outcomes for the experience, such as through a final prompt or cumulive learning survey. While *formative* and *summative assessments* are defined by when the assessment occurs, both forms are valid ways to collect and measure student learning as long as they are conducted when it is reasonable to expect students to demonstrate learning associated with a specific learning outcome.

Determining when to collect data requires educators to ask three basic questions. First, *how much time is needed to collect data?* A simple single question learning survey or writing prompt may take under 5 minutes to complete. Educators might need more time for longer or more complex learning surveys, writing prompts, and responses to scenarios. Additionally, using rubrics to observe student behavior may take more time from both students and the educator. Second, *how soon can students be expected to demonstrate learning?* Straightforward content, such as concept definitions or simple application of content to their lives, may be reasonable to assess during or at the end of an educational experience. It may not be reasonable to collect data about more complex content and content that requires deeper reflection or time for application, such as awareness of inequality in specific contexts or intergroup behaviors, right away. Student learning is not always linear and may require further opportunities for students to reflect and practice content (Keeling, 2004). In these cases, educators should consider how much time is necessary before they can reasonably expect students to demonstrate learning during future educational experiences or after these experiences have ended. Third, *how can students be incentivized to provide data?* When collecting data during the educational experience, the "incentive" may be to move onto the next activity. When collecting data at the end of the educational experience, be careful if data collection stands between them leaving, or else the received responses from students may be rushed. Educators might incentivize thoughtful responses through small prizes or candy. Collecting data from students after the educational experience has ended is trickiest if educators do not have access to these students again. In these cases, the incentive needs to be extra compelling. Asking students to submit responses to a physical office or online might be coupled with a raffle entry. If educators hosted a workshop or structured conversation with students as part of a class or job training, they could collaborate with faculty or staff to require students to complete and submit their responses.

An important and related topic to the timing of data collection is that of a pre-/post-test design. A pre-/post-test design is a specific approach to data collection

where educators collect the same data prior to and after an educational experience to observe a change in learning. Pre-/post-test designs are appealing because they are easy to understand and compelling. However, a pre-/post-test design is not always the best, or a necessary, approach to assess student learning. If the goal is to determine if students have demonstrated learning after an educational experience, collecting data once at the end of, or after, an educational experience is sufficient. If the goal is to claim a specific educational experience caused learning, then a pre-/post-test design would be appropriate. Most learning outcomes do not require a causal claim about where students learned, so carefully consider if the extra time and work required for collecting and analyzing data before *and* after an educational experience is necessary.

Step 5: Analyze and Use Your Data to Improve the Educational Experience

Once educators collect their data, they need to analyze and use it. When analyzing student learning data, the primary purpose is to determine how many students were successful in demonstrating learning. To answer this question, educators need to determine a threshold of success for their learning assessment. If educators distribute a five-question learning survey to students, how many questions should students answer correctly to meet expectations for learning? Similarly, if educators use a rubric with five criteria, how many criteria must students demonstrate to either meet or exceed expectations? When determining the threshold of success, educators should consider what is reasonable to expect from students and what they expect from the curriculum they designed. In addition to determining students' success, data analysis should also explore students' common misconceptions. Do multiple students tend to select the same wrong answer on a learning survey question? Do they provide similar incorrect answers on a writing prompt? Relatedly, do students omit a similar part of a response when answering a writing prompt? Examining students' misconceptions will provide useful insight into areas where students may need additional teaching to be successful.

After analyzing the data to determine how many students successfully demonstrated learning and areas of common misconceptions, educators should examine these results in consideration of the designed curriculum and what actually happened when they facilitated the experience. Were students successful at demonstrating learning because the educator was "on their game" as a facilitator, or because a specific activity was effective? Were students less successful at demonstrating learning because they had insufficient time to address a learning outcome or because the experience "took a left turn" away from the topic? Examining the results relative to how educators designed and implemented the educational experience is essential in order to decide what, if anything, they should change for the future. If a sufficient number of students demonstrated learning, the educator might decide that nothing needs to be changed. Such results might support them in making the experience available to more students. If students did not sufficiently demonstrate learning, the educator should make changes to the experience and collect more data to determine if those changes increased student learning.

Assessing student learning is important because educators should ensure they are effectively developing their students related to their intended learning outcomes. However, social justice educators should be further compelled to assess student learning to ensure that the curriculum sufficiently addresses the plurality of students. Social justice educators cannot adopt a "one-size-fits-all" approach to workshops or structured conversations because, as stated in chapter 1, students have different learning needs given their contextual influences. Therefore, assessing student learning provides important information to ensure education efforts are equitable for a diverse student body. Montenegro and Jankowski (2017) encourage a culturally responsive assessment approach that is mindful of how students' social identities and experiences shape their participation in learning assessment. Similar to considering the contextual influences that accounts for students' identities and experiences, culturally responsive assessment reminds educators to consider how data collection tools are developed and implemented and can skew results in favor of privileged groups. Educators should be mindful of the language used in developing learning outcomes and data collection tools, so students have clear expectations that guide their learning and responses to assessment. Further, the approach to data collection should not favor specific ways of demonstrating knowledge (e.g., written responses versus oral responses) when possible given other constraints that influence the approach.

While students may enter educational experiences at different places, educators have a responsibility to ensure they all grow.

While assessing social justice education takes time and effort, the process is beneficial.

I (Roger) believe in gathering data through well-thought evaluations that I create specific to programs, workshops, and experiences. I find this to be useful when not only communicating to students the value of their feedback but also presenting this information to key leaders on campus that can help advocate for the importance of this work and the benefit to students and the entire campus community. As stated earlier in this chapter, learning surveys, rubrics, and so on are extremely useful tools to assess programs. I find these especially useful when comparing responses to programs over a period of time (semester to semester and year to year). The data collected is useful to determine when it may be time to phase out certain programs and/or continue programs that maintain the enthusiasm of students and effectiveness of outcomes.

Additionally, I (Scott) have found creative ways to incorporate learning assessment into structured conversations and workshops to improve my teaching. When facilitating a series of structured conversations, I love asking students to complete a writing prompt on a note card at the end of the experience. Because structured conversations feel responsive to students' conversations, I frame the writing prompt in the context of our dialogue. Further, using note cards to collect data does not seem to intimidate students. Many students have told me they appreciate the chance to reflect in writing at the end of each session, and the size of the note card ensures that reflection is brief. My favorite thing to do is review the data and use the results to alter the curriculum for the next structured conversation. If students successfully demonstrated learning, I speak to their success in the introduction of the session. When students are not successful at demonstrating their learning, I share common misconceptions with the students and use that as an activity to further promote student learning before shifting into new content. Sometimes during these discussions I learn that I was unclear when teaching, and this provides a new opportunity to both promote learning and try a different approach to teaching that I can use next time. Using these "note card assessments" not only helps improve the curriculum and my facilitation practice but also provides me data to review the effectiveness of the structured dialogue series to observe how things are going each session and as an overall program.

When assessing a social justice education workshop or structured conversation, build the assessment approach around specific learning outcomes. Consider the following questions to ensure the approach will provide the information you need to improve the educational experience for each of the learning outcomes:

- What information do you need to collect to demonstrate student learning?
  - Does this information demonstrate knowledge, awareness, or behaviors?
  - Can student responses come from a predetermined list, their own words, or from witnessing their actions?
- What tools would best help you collect this information (e.g., learning survey, written prompt, rubric)?
- How much time is necessary to collect thoughtful responses from students?
- When is the most appropriate time to collect this information from students (during the experience, at the end of the experience, or after the experience)?
- How might students be incentivized to provide thoughtful responses?
- How do you plan to use the findings to improve either the curriculum or the facilitation?

Western College

It is possible to assess both learning outcomes for this workshop; however, it may be most pressing to assess the second learning outcome to ensure students have knowledge of respectful behaviors:

2. Identify communication strategies that respectfully explore how students express gender (intrapersonal behavior).

While this learning outcome focuses on students' behaviors, the way this outcome is written requires data that measures students' knowledge of behaviors, not their ability to demonstrate those behaviors.

Because this outcome requires students to identify only strategies, a simple one-question learning survey could be developed that asks students to identify communication strategies from a predetermined list that

FIGURE 6.3. Learning survey for learning outcome.

Which of the following communication strategies are helpful for respectful interactions related to gender pronouns? Select all that apply:	
Option A	Using pronouns for someone based on how they look to you
Option B	Asking someone what pronouns they use
Option C	Using someone's name instead of their pronouns
Option D	Avoiding interactions with others until you are certain of their pronouns
Option E	Asking other people about someone else's pronouns

models respectful interaction. The question could be asked using a multiple-answer format as shown in Figure 6.3.

To prevent students from repeating the correct answers they heard in the last activity of the workshop, this learning survey could be distributed to students either electronically or via slips of paper under their room door (a unique distribution method given the workshop happening in a residence hall) one week after the workshop occurred. If student completion is a concern, a small prize could be given to students who complete the learning survey. The results of this learning assessment could then inform future workshops that redress inaccurate knowledge or build on the content of the workshop.

Southeastern University

An essential step in the assessment process involves determining which student learning outcomes will be assessed. The first part of the four-part racial dialogue series has five total learning outcomes; however, assessing all five learning outcomes might take longer than an educator has time to implement. Therefore, they should identify those learning outcomes that are most essential for the experience. They might decide to assess the first two learning outcomes that create a foundation of knowledge essential for the entire dialogue series:

Students who participate in the first racial dialogue will be able to do the following:

1. Define concepts of *race, privilege, oppression,* and *racism.*

FIGURE 6.4. Writing prompt for learning outcome 1.

In your own words, please define each of the following concepts in one to two sentences: *privilege*, *oppression*, *race*, and *racism*.

Privilege	Oppression
Race	Racism

2. Describe how racial privilege and oppression influence the experience of racial groups in the United States.

A closer examination of these learning outcomes reveals that the educator needs to collect data about students' knowledge of concepts and awareness of racial power dynamics in their own words. The first learning outcome requires a straightforward definition of the concepts. The second learning outcome requires students to connect their knowledge about the concepts of privilege and oppression to race and the specific experiences of racial groups. The best method to collect and analyze both types of information are through a writing prompt and associated rubric.

The first learning outcome could be assessed using the following prompt: "In your own words, please define each of the following concepts in one to two sentences: *privilege*, *oppression*, *race*, and *racism*." To make it easier for students to complete, the educator could create a handout with this prompt and provide

space for each response to help students offer brief answers (see Figure 6.4).

A rubric would also be needed to assess students' responses based on the definitions taught during the dialogue. Without knowing the exact definitions taught in the dialogue, the generic rubric, which highlights the importance of knowing central ideas that vary for each definition, could be used (see Table 6.3).

Because the facilitator would post the definitions for these terms in the space for students to see during the experience, this handout could be given to students at the start of the *second* dialogue when the definitions are not posted. Collecting this data at the start of the second dialogue could also become a useful activity to check students' knowledge and clarify misconceptions before beginning new content.

The prompt for the second learning outcome requires more direction to help students respond, such as "Given your understanding of privilege and oppression, provide at least one example for how racial privilege and oppression influence the experience of racial groups. Please be specific about how privilege and oppression affect different racial groups." While students could write about this topic at great length, students could be given note cards to encourage condensed responses. The associated rubric to assess students' responses would examine their ability to provide specific examples that they accurately applied to the concepts of privilege and oppression as well as to specific racial groups (see Table 6.4).

This outcome could be assessed at the end of the first dialogue in order to build on the conversations had about racial privilege and oppression and help the facilitator glean how well students understood the content to guide any revisions for the second dialogue in the series.

TABLE 6.3. Generic Rubric for Learning Outcome 1

	Below Expectations	*Meets Expectations*	*Exceeds Expectations*
Definition of Privilege	Student incorrectly defines *privilege or* provides a definition of *privilege* that is missing at least one central idea	Student correctly defines *privilege* and includes all central ideas in their definition	Student correctly defines *privilege*, includes all central ideas in their definition, *and* expands on at least one of these central ideas

TABLE 6.4. Rubric for Learning Outcome 2

	Below Expectations	*Meets Expectations*	*Exceeds Expectations*
Identification of Example	Student does not provide an example *or* provides an irrelevant example	Student provides *one* relevant example	Student provides *more than one* relevant example
Connection to Privilege and Oppression	The connection to *both* concepts are either missing, unclear, or inaccurate	The connection to *both* concepts is clear and accurate but *implicit*	The connection to *both* concept are clear, accurate, and *explicit*
Connection to Racial Groups	The connection to racial groups is missing, unclear, or inaccurate	The connection to racial groups is clear and accurate but *implicit*	The connection to racial groups is clear, accurate, and *explicit*

Handout 6.1
Reflecting on Assessing Student Learning

Think about each step in the assessment process and draft your plan:

1. What learning outcomes will be assessed?

2. Given your learning outcomes, what data do you need and from whom?

Data needed:

a.

b.

c.

d.

Data collected from:

3. What tools are needed to collect and analyze data? Check each tool you need and state which types of data on the left will be collected from each tool you plan to use.

☐ Learning survey

☐ Writing prompt

☐ Rubric

4a. When will you collect your data?

☐ During the experience

☐ At the end of the experience

☐ After the experience

When: _____

4b. How will you incentivize data collection?

5a. When analyzing your data, what will be your threshold for success?

5b. When will you make time to analyze and interpret your data to improve the experience?

CHAPTER 7

Considerations for Online Experiences

Educators often design social justice education workshops and structured conversations for in-person implementation. However, technology has helped evolve the educational landscape toward online teaching and learning in multiple ways. Technology has enabled educators to facilitate distance learning experiences, fully online courses and workshops, and blended in-person and online experiences (Bowen, 2012; Kearsley, 2005; Rudestam & Schoenholtz-Read, 2010; Stephenson, 2001). *Online education* is an umbrella term that encompasses the use of technology to support teaching and learning in both real-time and asynchronous formats. Online education may include software that connects two in-person spaces, teleconferencing platforms (e.g., Google Meet, Skype, Zoom), learning management systems (e.g., Blackboard, Canvas, D2L), and online modules designed to teach content. While some educators find value and promise in online education (Reif, 2013), others are skeptical of the impact it can have on social justice outcomes and educational equity (Bonilla, 2011). Educators committed to providing students with social justice education experiences must ask themselves to what extent they are able and willing to adapt their curriculum, facilitation, and assessment for virtual education spaces.

We believe in-person social justice education workshops and structured conversations are powerful and preferable. However, we also believe that our preferences should not prevent educators from considering the conditions under which social justice education can be successful. If educators refuse to engage social justice education in online spaces, they jeopardize the longevity of our work in a changing landscape and prevent students from learning. Online learning

provides a variety of unique opportunities that can support students' learning about social justice education. For example, online formats often rely on a greater amount of explicit student participation that may also increase feelings of vulnerability given the distance among the students (Domingue, 2016). Blended workshops that incorporate online modules for students to complete prior to an in-person workshop can provide students with foundational content knowledge in an online space, resulting in more time for task-based and discussion-based activities during the in-person workshop (Tharp, 2017). Online videos can facilitate learning through lecture-based content, sharing stories, and taking students on "field trips" to show them realities they might not typically experience (Costa, 2020). With our imaginations open to the possibility of online experiences, let us consider how to adapt each step in the process of designing, facilitation, and assessing social justice education workshops and structured conversations for online learning environments.

Contextual Influences

While the contextual influences discussed in chapter 1 are still relevant, educators must consider additional issues related to online experiences. These additional issues relate to the level of visibility of individuals' social identities, degree of students' familiarity with online technologies and software platforms, and the variability that exists in creating and maintaining educational spaces online. Using the framework discussed in chapter 1, these additional contextual issues relate to educators themselves, the students, and the environment when preparing an online social justice education experience.

First, educators should remember that online spaces can influence how educators see themselves and express their social identities. For example, if educators use technology that enables face-to-face interactions, their most visual social identities may become more salient and that may influence how they enact their social identities in the space with their students. However, if educators use technology that does not show who they are, educators will have greater control over which social identities they make explicit and how they bring their social identities into the space.

Second, educators should also reflect on how students' prior knowledge and motivation to participate in online education spaces are relevant. Students' familiarity with online learning in general and specific online software platforms can influence how much effort educators need to spend when preparing students to participate effectively in an online space. Students' familiarity with online learning and specific technologies or platforms could create barriers for learning if educators do not consider these items. Relatedly, educators would need to consider the ways both real-time and asynchronous formats, along with specific online technologies or software platforms, would influence the quantity and quality of student participation. For example, using technology for face-to-face interaction in a real-time format may increase student participation while a discussion board feature on a learning management system in an asynchronous format may reduce student participation.

Third, online education experiences inspire further reflection on the educational environment. Given the multitude of ways educators can facilitate online learning, they should consider how the formats and technologies used in the educational experience contribute to the learning environment. Real-time formats versus asynchronous formats can influence the ways student dynamics appear in the space along with the amount of time educators provide for students to engage meaningfully with the content and one another.

Theories and Conceptual Frameworks

Developing social justice education workshops and structured conversations for an online experience does not influence how educators reflect on relevant theories and conceptual frameworks. Theories and conceptual frameworks help educators clarify their approach to social justice education given students' developmental needs. The frameworks educators choose should not change based on delivering an online or in-person education experience. If educators believe that the MOD framework is relevant to promote student learning related to systemic privilege and oppression, developing an education experience in an online format does not negate the need for students to learn about systemic privilege and oppression.

Cultural Consciousness and Learning Outcomes

Given the additional contextual influences relevant to online technologies and formats, educators may need to modify which learning goals they prioritize for online social justice education experiences. In most cases, online education experiences can effectively contribute to most learning content using the matrix of cultural consciousness discussed in chapter 3. Learning goals situated within the knowledge domain of learning are the most transferable for online experiences. The development of students' awareness is also transferable to most online spaces; however, some educators may be less likely to prioritize awareness at the communal and interpersonal social levels if they believe those learning goals require in-person experiential learning. Similarly, educators may believe that prioritizing the development of students' behaviors is less effective if students cannot sufficiently practice these behaviors in an online setting.

To clarify how online technologies and formats influence educators' prioritization of learning outcomes, let us consider the development of dialogue skills with one's peers as a specific interpersonal behavior. Teleconference platforms that allow real-time, face-to-face interactions may provide opportunities to develop skills for dialogue among students. Asynchronous discussion boards may be less effective at facilitating the development of dialogue skills; however, they could help promote different interpersonal skills specific to text-based interactions through social media platforms or text messaging. Online modules completed prior to a live workshop might be useful to teach knowledge of dialogue skills that students could practice during an in-person experience. These different examples highlight how the formats and technologies used can shape how educators prioritize specific learning goals for their social justice education experience.

Pedagogical Considerations and Selecting Activities

Educators' commitment to the principles of social justice education remains equally as important for in-person and online education experiences. However, online education does require extra consideration for the fifth principle of establishing a welcoming and inclusive environment.

Educators should consider creating additional guidelines specific to the online environment and explain how those guidelines will be actively maintained. For asynchronous formats where discussion posts are not monitored regularly, as well as real-time formats using teleconferencing technology where the educator cannot monitor all students at one time, these additional guidelines are especially important. Educators might also create a video introduction they post for students to view first as part of an asynchronous experience. A video introduction provides a way for educators to build a relationship with their students while also reminding everyone that there are people on the other end of their computer screen (Costa, 2020).

The extra considerations related to contextual influences and the learning goals that inform the learning outcomes for the education experience will also influence the activities educators select. For blended experiences where educators ask students to complete online modules prior to an in-person workshop, educators benefit from the additional online space that creates more time for task-based and discussion-based activities. However, for other online experiences using either real-time or asynchronous formats, educators will need to consider which conditions are most effective for task-based and discussion-based activities. Many task-based activities normally implemented during an in-person workshop or structured dialogue may require some creativity or modification for an online space.

Let us consider the example of the line-up icebreaker shared in chapter 5. This symbolic task-based activity, which is designed to illuminate students' assumptions and replicate feelings of social marginalization, depends on students being in the same physical space so that limiting their vocal interaction forces them to find other ways to communicate with one another while forming a line based on where they live. While educators cannot recreate this activity as is, they could modify it for different formats and technologies. Educators using a real-time format with teleconferencing technology could ask students to not verbally talk and force them to use visual cues to communication with one another. Further, educators could indicate their "location in line" by using their hands to indicate a number for each person. If educators use a real-time format with a discussion board, they could instruct students to communicate with one another using only three characters at a time when they type during their interaction. Students could then type their number to indicate their place "in line." Both of these modifications allow educators to achieve the same goal through creative instructions.

While this example of how to modify a task-based activity is useful for real-time formats, some activities are less transferable for online spaces. Let us consider a different example of the privilege walk activity that was also discussed in chapter 5. This simulation task-based activity designed to replicate social stratification depends on students being in the same physical space to observe where students stand relative to one another. While educators cannot easily reconstruct this activity in an online environment, educators can explore other ways to accomplish the same goal. For example, educators might encourage students to have a similar experience through an introspective task-based activity such as asking students to read a list of privilege walk statements, adding or subtracting points for each statement with which they agreed, and then being ready to discuss their experience.

Educators need to consider different issues for discussion-based activities than those presented related to task-based activities. Whereas educators may need to modify, recreate, or substitute task-based activities, discussion-based activities can still occur as originally intended. However, educators should take into account the types of questions they ask students based on the format and technology of the online experience. Discussion-based activities that include more questions that may cause students to feel vulnerable, such as questions about their social identity–based experiences related to discrimination, may not be appropriate in an online discussion board or as part of an asynchronous format. Students may reasonably feel uncomfortable sharing their experiences without the ability to see how other students are reacting in real-time. Silence from others students can be damaging to the student who shared and dampen other students' willingness to share. Therefore, educators should reflect carefully on the level of risk they are asking students to take by answering a question depending on the nature of the online experience.

Facilitation

The facilitation of online social justice education workshops and structured conversations requires a few additional considerations related to educators' self-work and specific facilitation skills. First, when preparing for an online education experience, educators self-work should include reflecting on their interpersonal style and the ways it may be different in an online setting versus an in-person setting. For example, it is possible that some educators prefer informal communication preferences during in-person experiences but have formal communication preferences in an online environment to bring more order and structure to the engagement. A second area of self-work on which educators should reflect is related to their comfort with silence. Depending on the online format and technology, student silence may refer to verbal or written contributions in a real-time format as well as delays between written comments during an asynchronous format. Educators should consider how student silence makes them feel, how they interpret that silence, and how reasonable their expectations for student participation are that may contribute to silence. Third, educators should take time to consider whether or not their existing triggers look different in online spaces and whether or not online environments contribute to additional triggers they would not normally think about in their facilitation.

Educators will need to modify their facilitation skills related to creating relationships with students, listening and observing, soliciting participation, and reading the room. The ways in which educators employ these skills will look different depending on

the technologies and software platforms used in the experience. Online experiences using teleconferencing technology still allows for verbal communication; however, the ability to express and attend to non-verbal behaviors will be limited based on how many students can see one another at a given time. For example, using Zoom teleconference software on a computer allows educators to see all students on a single screen. However, using Zoom on a mobile phone allows you to view up to only four people at a time. Therefore, educators' ability to connect to students, as well as listen and observe them, may be limited, thus reducing their ability to read the room and invite students to participate. In this type of online setting, educators may consider asking students to use different forms of verbal expression to provide feedback, such as affirmation snaps or using gestures to communicate feelings, to provide them with cues to help them navigate the experience.

Text-based interactions through discussion boards pose an even greater challenge to expressing and observing non-verbal behaviors and the tone behind what has been shared. In this context, educators are truly limited to being able to see what students explicitly write, leaving much unsaid. In this setting, educators will need to use other tools in their toolbox to solicit explicit engagement. For example, an educator may ask students to share their reactions using a "1 to 5" rating scale to read the room and solicit student participation based on their ranking. Educators might also need to use the skills of responding to students with questions to generate more explicit comments and feelings that might be more noticeable during an in-person experience.

Assessing Student Learning

The five steps for assessing student learning remain the same for both in-person and online education experience. The process always begins with identifying the learning outcomes statement the educator wants to assess. Therefore, the data needed to be collected from students, the tools needed to collect and analyze that data, and the importance of analyzing and using the data does not change. However, the specific ways educators choose to collect data from students may need slight modification because paper and pencil approaches are not an option. Learning surveys can be easily created and distributed online using any number of survey platforms or quiz templates embedded in learning management software platforms. Written prompts are also easy to implement and receive online. However, educators may need to modify how they introduce and collect written prompts from their students.

For example, imagine an educator was facilitating a structured dialogue using a real-time discussion board online and wanted to incorporate a short writing prompt midway through the session. The educator could still share the writing prompt with students by posting the question to students in the discussion. However, because an online discussion board replicates an in-person discussion, educators would not want students to post their replies in the discussion thread for other students to see. If that happened, students could easily copy and paste what someone else typed or not answer at all if someone else says something too similar to what they thought. To avoid this challenge, educators would need to create a different mechanism for students to submit their short answers. Educators could create a simple survey with one open-ended question and post the link in the discussion board for students to click on and enter their replies.

Same Process, Different Format

Walking through the six steps related to social justice education curricula design, facilitation, and assessment shows how this process is still relevant and useful for online education. The main differences between an in-person and online experience revolve around the format and technologies used in the experience. Before developing or modifying a social justice education workshop or structured conversation for an online experience, consider the following questions:

- Will this workshop or structured conversation be offered as a blended or fully online experience?
- Will students participate in the experience in real-time or asynchronously?
- What technology and software platforms are available to you and your students that can facilitate learning?
- Will students have access to the necessary technology (e.g., computer, internet, webcam) to participate in an online experience?
- How familiar are you and your students with the technology and software platforms you intend to use to facilitate learning?

PART TWO

EXAMPLES OF APPLYING THIS PROCESS TO SOCIAL JUSTICE EDUCATION WORKSHOPS AND STRUCTURED CONVERSATIONS

CHAPTER 8

Introductory Diversity Workshop at Large Midwestern University (LMU)

Large Midwestern University (LMU) requires all first-year students to enroll in a first-year seminar class in the fall term. This class includes a traditional course component led by a faculty member and a college transitions seminar led by a student peer mentor that occurs every week. The curriculum for the college transitions seminar includes an hour-long session on diversity and social justice. I (Scott) designed the diversity and social justice session for student peer mentors to lead these sessions; however, guest speakers (including myself) could also be invited to facilitate sessions.

Contextual Influences

The following were relevant to consider prior to developing the curriculum for this workshop:

Yourself, the Educator

My social identities and related experiences in college as non-Christian, working class, and White collectively influenced my approach to this session. As a first-year college student, my most salient identity was being non-Christian and working class, which masked my awareness about my Whiteness and ability to analyze race. However, when educators and mentors helped me think about race through the lens of social class and religion, I became open to examining race in new ways. Therefore, as an educator developing this session, my memory of these experiences profoundly shaped my desire to create an experience that allowed

students to engage the topic through any identity that resonated most with themselves. Similarly, these identities were most salient to me when facilitating this session, influencing the types of examples I would share and how I tried to build relationships with students.

Student Influences

This diversity and social justice session impacted roughly 2,400 first-year students across 110 courses. Therefore, broad assumptions could not be made about what these students needed because of the demographic make-up of the first-year student body. Their academic majors varied, with many being undecided. The diversity of social identities present within the first-year student body included students of color (35%), females (55%), first-generation college students (40%), and students who were non-Christian (30%). While LMU did not collect information about students' sexuality, it historically attracts students who identify as lesbian, gay, bisexual, transgender, and queer (LGBTQ). While this diversity of students was true for the entire first-year student body, each session did not proportionally represent this blend of students.

The students' prior knowledge about diversity and social justice varied widely given that students enrolled from a blend of public and private high schools in urban, suburban, and rural communities across the United States and internationally. It was likely that many students had engaged with people different from their own social identities. At the same time, a considerable proportion of students had come from homogenous backgrounds. However, all of these students would have completed a few shared experiences prior to the diversity and social justice session in the fall term. First, they completed a new student orientation experience that introduced them to concepts of diversity, social identity, and intergroup dynamics. Second, their first-year seminar discusses the mission of LMU with explicit attention to the importance of diversity. Third, all of these first-year seminar courses explored at least one aspect of social diversity in the urban area where LMU is located.

The diversity and social justice sessions' placement within a required first-year seminar course influenced student motivation to participate. Students were required to attend the session as part of their class. Additionally, the course instructors graded students on their participation, which made students more likely to engage actively in the session.

Environment Influences

The relevant educational context was linked to both the first-year seminar course and the broader college transitions seminar curriculum in which the diversity and social justice session is embedded. Both of these elements shaped students' prior knowledge. The traditional course component of the seminar requires all students to experience multiple aspects of the local urban environment that exposes them to explicit racial and socioeconomic disparities in the community. While faculty were taught the session curriculum in advance and were highly encouraged to integrate its content throughout their course, the faculty range in their desire to focus on social identity and related disparities as a focal point for learning. Additionally, the diversity and social justice session lasted an hour and occurred any time after the first week of the course. Therefore, it was highly likely that students would bring their knowledge and experiences from the class into the session. Last, the fact that the students were new to college and looking to fit in and find a sense of belonging among their peers likely shaped student dynamics during the session. Therefore, these group dynamics likely influenced student participation in the session.

Student interaction with the campus environment at this point was limited to their experiences during the summer new student orientation and the first weeks of their first term on campus. Few incidents were reported during this period of time that jeopardized campus climate. Further, most first-year students report high perceptions of safety on campus on the National Survey of Student Engagement (NSSE). While campus environment concerns were limited, it is important to note that marginalized groups often don't report microaggressions from both peers and faculty that they may have experienced.

Influences from the broader social environment were quite relevant. The university is located in a highly racially segregated urban environment. This urban environment was also nationally known for having a vibrant LGBTQ and religiously diverse community. National attention around Black Lives Matter, police brutality, gun violence, and living wages were also topics that were likely present and influenced the consciousness of these students.

Theories and Conceptual Frameworks

The contextual influences identified were addressed using multiple theories and conceptual frameworks to develop the session. Specifically, the plurality of students required a framework that could address a wide range of social identities, experiences, and prior knowledge. Because no assumptions could be made about the students attending any given session, frameworks that could sufficiently address the shared experiences of these students were limited. The students could serve as a launching point that taps into current events or timely topics presented through their shared educational experience in the course.

Three frameworks were integrated to create the curriculum. First, DMIS was valuable given the varied educational experiences of students in high school coupled with the desire to create a solid foundation for future educational experiences on campus. It seemed critical for students to acknowledge diversity and adopt an ethnorelative paradigm to effectively engage in broader conversations on privilege and oppression. Second, SIDM was useful when considering how to engage students who recognize social differences but might also have an underdeveloped understanding of social inequality. Given the multitude of social identities that may be present among students in any given workshop, I-MMDI was critical to conceptualize activities to engage all students using their existing knowledge and experiences that they could then connect to new content on diversity and social justice.

Cultural Consciousness and Learning Outcomes

A 60-minute session required strategic selection of learning content areas for student learning across the different domains of learning, social levels, and social identities. Knowledge and awareness were the primary domains of learning, given the goal of this session to provide foundational knowledge on diversity and social justice. Additionally, a focus on the intrapersonal and communal levels of learning would allow participants to deeply reflect on their lives and apply foundational knowledge to their lived experiences. Because of the diversity of social identities in the student population, coupled with the uncertainty of representation during any given workshop, no single social identity group was the focus. Instead, the goal was to encourage students to think about any number of social identities depending on their own most salient social identities.

The focus on knowledge and awareness domains of learning across the intrapersonal and communal levels through the lens of any social identity inspired the formation of two learning outcomes:

Students who participate in the diversity and social justice session will do the following:

1. Define and apply core concepts of *diversity*, *social identity*, *privilege*, and *oppression*.
2. Identify and describe their own social identities and related experiences.

The first learning outcome attended to the knowledge and awareness domain across the intrapersonal and communal levels. The second learning outcome attended to the awareness domain across the intrapersonal, interpersonal, and communal levels. Additionally, the second learning outcome invited students to engage any social identity they choose. These learning outcomes supported students' ability to both develop their awareness of diversity through their personal social identities and explore the relationship between their identity-based experiences and systems of privilege and oppression. These goals aligned with the intentions of all three frameworks previously identified.

The formulation of these learning outcomes satisfied the expectations of a well-written outcome statement. The outcomes were meaningful for an introductory diversity session and were written at an appropriate level that require students to demonstrate basic knowledge and comprehension, a reasonable task after a 60-minute session. Both outcomes used actions verbs ("define and apply," "identify and describe") that were connected to explicit learning tasks that were observable and measurable based on what a student writes or says. Last, the content of these outcomes were clear, leaving little ambiguity about what the focus of learning is and what is expected from students.

Pedagogical Considerations and Activities

The following two-part blended curriculum was developed to achieve both learning outcomes developed for this experience. The first part involved a short 5-minute online module. The second part involved a live 60-minute session.

The online module was essentially a lecture activity that students could complete asynchronously. The module taught students about the definitions of six core concepts: *diversity, social identity, privilege, oppression, social justice,* and *allyship*. The module provided definitions for each concept and explained how these concepts relate to one another. Course instructors asked students to complete this online module prior to the 60-minute session.

The 60-minute session consisted of six primary activities. After a few minutes introducing the facilitator and the content for the session, the first 5-minute activity involved reviewing guidelines for conversation previously established for the course and making explicit how and why these guidelines were relevant to the session. Second was a 7-minute introspective activity where students completed an identity wheel (modified from Bell, Love, & Roberts, 2007) about multiple social identities of their choosing. This activity asked students to identify specific values, experiences, and traditions related to each social identity. Third was an 8-minute discussion pair activity where students shared and discussed their identity wheel with a peer. Fourth was a 15-minute large group discussion activity where students reflected on the process of completing their identity wheels and discussing them with a peer. This activity allowed the facilitator to actively highlight key ideas and insights related to the core concepts taught in the online module and normalize the benefits of talking about one's social identities with one another. The fifth activity was 20 minutes of combined lecture and large group discussion that focused on reviewing the core concepts covered in the online module while also using structured prompts to connect their understanding of these concepts to the course and their personal lives. This flexibly designed activity built on students' prior knowledge based on both course content and experiences. The sixth activity involved a brief lecture activity that allowed the facilitator to highlight key ideas and takeaways from the entire session and address lingering questions students had.

The activities across the session curriculum collectively addressed all five principles for social justice education. Students intentionally developed knowledge, awareness, and behaviors (specifically defined by the two learning outcomes) from both the online module and the identity wheel activity and related discussion pair and large group discussion activities. Students' prior knowledge and experiences were actively solicited during the identity wheel activity and applied during large group discussion activities. Students' positionalities were explored most directly in the identity wheel activity and the follow-up discussion pair activity. However, students' emotions and thoughts were directly engaged during the large group discussion about the identity wheels when facilitators asked students how it felt to complete their identity wheel and share it with a peer. Last, an inclusive and welcoming environment was established by timing the session to occur after the first week of the course to allow more time for students to get to know one another better and through the guidelines for conversation activity at the start of the session.

Assessing Student Learning

Both learning outcomes were critical to assess for this learning experience. In order to assess both learning outcomes, data was needed from students who participated in the session. Specifically, this necessary data related to (a) students' understanding of privilege and oppression (as the most critical core concepts), (b) students' ability to identify and describe their own social identities, and (c) students' ability to apply their understanding of privilege and oppression to their own social identities. Because this necessary data is different for each student, a writing prompt and rubric were created to collect and analyze students' data. Course instructors distributed the following writing prompt to students at the end of the session and informed them to submit their responses in 2 weeks' time for course credit:

> In 1 to 2 pages, explicitly reflect on both concepts of privilege and oppression as discussed in today's class session, and think about them in light of at least two of the social identities you reflected on in your identity wheel. How might your social identities relate to these concepts? How do these concepts help you explain or understand your social identities and related experiences? How might they influence the way you engage in conversations about diversity with other students on campus? Your response should reflect an accurate definition of both concepts using concrete examples (beyond mere description) from your personal experiences related to your identities. If needed, the online module, along with digital copies of the core concepts handout and identity wheel handout, can all be found on our course website.

Data was analyzed using an internally created rubric with two domains that corresponded with each learning outcome (see Table 8.1). Successful student learning was achieved if students meet or exceeded expectations in for each domain.

TABLE 8.1. Rubric for Diversity Session

	Below Expectations	*Meets Expectations*	*Exceeds Expectations*
Knowledge of Core Concepts	Student does not demonstrate an accurate understanding of privilege *and* oppression per the lesson plan curriculum	Student demonstrates an accurate understanding of *either* privilege or oppression per the lesson plan curriculum	Student demonstrates an accurate understanding of *both* privilege and oppression per the lesson plan curriculum
Application of Core Concepts to Social Identities	Student identifies fewer than two social identities *or* inaccurately applied privilege or oppression to their identities	Student explicitly identifies two social identities *and* accurately applies *either* privilege or oppression to their identities	Student explicitly identifies two social identities *and* accurately applies *both* privilege and oppression to their identities

Handout 8.1
Reflecting on Contextual Influences:
Yourself, the Educator

1. Identify your social identities and circle those that you believe are most salient to this workshop or structured conversation.

   a. Race: **White**

   b. Ethnicity: **German**

   c. Sex: **Male**

   d. Gender: **Cisgender man**

   e. Sexual orientation: **Heterosexual**

   f. Ability status: **Able-bodied**

   g. Religion or faith: **Non-Christian**

   h. Social class: **Raised working class; currently middle class**

   i. Other:

   j. Other:

2. How do you enact your most salient social identities?

Having a heightened awareness of my racial identity makes me more conscious about the racial plurality of students in every session. I am increasingly conscious about how students of color participate in the session. Therefore, I make extra attempts to bring their voice into the experience to model how White folks can share space with people of color.

My social class identity influences me to adopt a relatively informal facilitation style to ensure students view me as approachable. I use my facilitation style to offset how students may perceive me because my workplace requires me to wear business professional attire. Additionally, I use slang and speech patterns viewed as "incorrect" that reflect my experience growing up to connect to students who may share a similar social identity.

3. How might your salient social identities impact your facilitation?

My experiences through my intersectional race and social class identities influence my desire to connect to students' oppressed social identities in order to help them understand their privileged social identities.

Reflecting on Contextual Influences:
Student and Environmental Influences

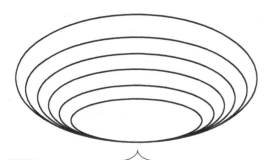

When considering student influences:

4. What *demographics* are present among the students that might be most relevant to the workshop or structured conversation?

The first-year student body includes a sizable proportion of students of color (35%), females (55%), first-generation college students (40%), and non-Christians (30%), increasing the likelihood of students in each session holding multiple different social identities.

5. What prior *knowledge* or relevant formal or informal education experiences have these students shared prior to this workshop or structured conversation, and how might that shape how different students engage the experience?

Students will have had (a) a summer orientation that introduces them to diversity terms and intergroup dynamics and (b) some conversation about differences related to the local urban area in their course.

6. What might *motivate* different students to attend or fully participate in this workshop or structured conversation, and how might that shape the nature of their participation?

Students are required to participate in the session because it is embedded in a required course where students receive a grade for participation.

When considering environmental influences:

7. How might *educational* factors, including prior content covered, existing group dynamics, and the duration of the experience, shape the workshop or structured conversation?

The session is limited to 60 minutes; however, it will build on previous conversations about social differences in the course. The session must occur after the second week of the term to allow social relationships to develop among new students.

8. What recent *campus* events or potential campus climate concerns might different students have that are relevant to how they perceive or experience the workshop or structured conversation?

Students are new and have limited experiences on campus prior to the session. While first-year students report high levels of satisfaction with campus climate, experiences from oppressed student communities are likely underreported.

9. What relevant recent *off-campus* issues at the local, state, or national levels might influence different students' perceptions of or experience during the workshop or structured conversation?

The local urban area is extremely racially segregated, has a vibrant LGBTQ community, and is religiously diverse. National attention related to Black Lives Matter, police brutality, gun violence, and living wages are common topics likely to be present.

Handout 8.2
Reflecting on Theories and Conceptual Frameworks Relative to Contextual Influences

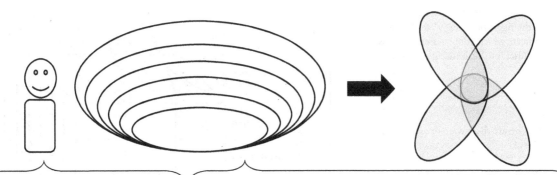

1. Which theories or frameworks resonate the most with you and your approach to social justice education?

Social identity development model

2. How might your social identities and related experiences influence the theories or conceptual frameworks that you default to using in this work?

My experience as an undergraduate student learning about my privilege through the lens of my oppressed social identities aligns with the developmental trajectory described by the social identity development model.

3. Which theories or conceptual frameworks seem useful given what you know about the students, specifically related to the following:

a. Demographics

   Developmental model of intercultural sensitivity

b. Prior knowledge

   Intersectional model of multiple dimensions of identity

c. Motivation to participate

   Social identity development model

4. Which theories or conceptual frameworks seem useful given the environment, specifically related to the following:

a. Expectations from stakeholders for the workshop or structured conversation

   Developmental model of intercultural sensitivity

b. Amount of time you have for the workshop or structured conversation

   Developmental model of intercultural sensitivity

c. Relevant issues on campus or from the broader social environment that may be pressing on students

   Intersectional model of multiple dimensions of identity

Handout 8.3
Reflecting on Cultural Consciousness Content Areas and Learning Outcomes

1. Using the matrix of cultural consciousness to the right, place an "x" in the squares to indicate which content areas are most essential for this learning experience.

2. Why are these content areas most essential?

This session provides a common foundation about differences and social power for students to build on during their time on campus. Therefore, the focus for the session should be on knowledge and awareness about themselves and others related to multiple social identities.

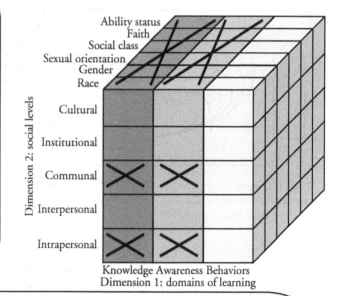

3. For each content area identified, transform it into a single learning outcome statement. For each learning outcome statement, ensure it includes all three parts and satisfies the seven best practices for writing learning outcomes:

_____**First-year students**_____ who _____**participate in the diversity session during the fall term**_____
      (Audience)   (Condition)

will be able to:

Behavior a.   **Define and apply core concepts of *diversity*, *social identity*, *privilege*, and *oppression***

Behavior b.   **Identify and describe their own social identities and related experiences**

Behavior checklist:
- ✓ Meaningful
- ✓ Tied to learning
- ✓ Uses action verbs
- ✓ Observable
- ✓ Measurable
- ✓ Written at an appropriate level
- ✓ Clear and concise

Handout 8.4
Reflecting on Pedagogical Considerations and Activities
(Building an Outline)

1. List your learning outcomes.

a. Define and apply core concepts of *diversity*, *social identity*, *privilege* and *oppression* (addressed by activities a, e, and f)

b. Identify and describe their own social identities and related experiences (addressed by activities c–f)

2. Create an outline for your workshop or structured conversation that identifies specific activities, approximate time durations, and specific discussion questions for discussion-based activities.

a. Lecture activity: Online module (5 minutes)

b. Guidelines for conversation (5 minutes)

c. Introspective activity: Identity wheel (7 minutes)

d. Discussion pair activity (8 minutes)
- In what ways do you embody diversity through your social identities?
- What do you notice about your partner's identity wheel?

e. Large group discussion activity (15 minutes)
- How was it to talk to your partner about your identity wheel?
- What insights did you gain from either drawing your identity wheel or the discussion with your partner?
- Why do you think it is important to talk about diversity and our social identities at LMU?

f. Lecture/large group discussion activity (20 minutes)
- Were there things that came out in your dialogue on your identity wheel that relate to privilege or oppression? If so, which ones and how?
- What examples of privilege or oppression did you notice when creating your identity wheels?
- What examples of privilege did you see during the class/field trips?
- What examples of oppression did you see during the class/field trips?

g. Lecture activity: Highlight key takeaways (5 minutes)

Five principles

#1: Facilitate the development of knowledge, awareness, and behaviors **(addressed by activities a, c–g)**

#2: Utilize students' knowledge and experiences **(addressed by activities c–f)**

#3: Help students understand their positionality within systems of inequality **(addressed by activities c–e)**

#4: Engage emotional and cognitive aspects of learning **(addressed by activities c–e, g)**

#5: Establish a welcoming and inclusive environment **(addressed by activity b)**

3. State which activities address both (a) the learning outcomes on the left and (b) the principles on the right. Modify your outline until it addresses all of your learning outcomes and principles for social justice education

Handout 8.5
Reflecting on Assessing Student Learning

Think about each step in the assessment process and draft your plan:

1. What learning outcome(s) will be assessed?

   Define and apply core concepts of *diversity*, *social identity*, *privilege*, and *oppression*. Identify and describe their own social identities and related experiences.

2. Given your learning outcomes, what data do you need, and from whom?

   Data needed:

   a. Students' understanding of privilege and oppression

   b. Students' ability to identify and describe their own social identities

   c. Students' ability to apply their understanding of privilege and oppression to their own social identities

   Data collected from:

   Students who participated in the session

3. What tools are needed to collect and analyze data? Check each tool you need and state which types of data on the left will be collected from each tool you plan to use.

   ☐ Learning survey

   ✓ **Writing prompt (a, b, c)**

   ✓ **Rubric**

4a. When will you collect your data?

   ☐ During the experience

   ☐ At the end of the experience

   ✓ **After the experience**

   When: **2 weeks after**

4b. How will you incentivize data collection?

   Required as part of their grade

5a. When analyzing your data, what will be your threshold for success?

   Students must meet or exceed expectations for all domains of the rubric.

5b. When will you make time to analyze and interpret your data to improve the experience?

   After the end of the fall term

Handout 8.6
Social Identity Wheel

Create your social identity wheel by creating different-sized sections that reflect how much you think about each social identity. In each slice of the wheel, draw pictures or write words that represent your personal values, traditions, histories, or experiences related that social identity (e.g., traditions related to ethnicity, experiences around gender, values related to your social class).

Personality traits or characteristics are not considered social identities.

1. Race/ethnicity

2. Gender identity

3. Sexual orientation

4. Religion/spirituality

5. Social class

6. Ability status

7. Other identities

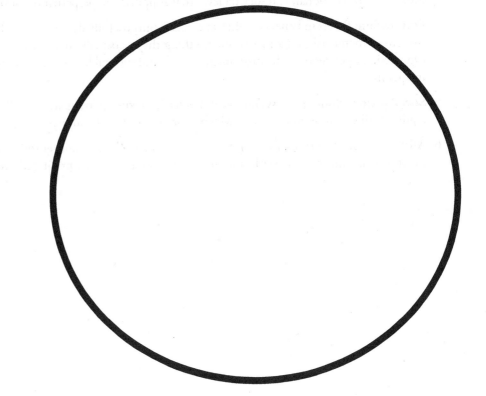

After, find a partner and talk about your identity wheel by answering the following question: "In what ways do I embody diversity through my social identities?" After you share, your partner will reflect back to you three significant things they noticed while you were sharing.

Core Concepts

1. **Diversity**: The differences among people reflected through personal experiences, historical legacies, and treatment, which are based on social identities. Not the same as differences or "being different."

2. **Social identity**: The way a person defines themselves relative to sociocultural group memberships (e.g., race, social class, gender, faith/religion, ability status, sexual orientation). This does not include personality traits or characteristics (e.g., a "son/daughter," friendly, hardworking).

3. **Privilege**: Refers to unearned benefits, rights, and access granted to people based on their social identity group membership. Not based on anything they personally have done or accomplished. Operates on an individual, institutional, and societal level that supports the perpetuation of social inequality.

4. **Oppression**: Refers to benefits, rights, and access purposefully denied to people based on their social identity group membership. Not based on anything they personally have or have not done or accomplished. Oppression operates on individual, institutional, and societal levels that support the perpetuation of social inequality.

5. **Social justice**: Both a process and a goal that leads to equal participation of all groups in society along with equitable distribution of resources, which promotes physical and psychological safety.

6. **Ally**: A person who takes action against social injustice by promoting social change at the interpersonal, institutional, and systemic levels. Often an ally is a member of a privileged social identity group.

CHAPTER 9

Racial Literacy Dialogue for Small Liberal Arts College (SLAC)

Small Liberal Arts College (SLAC) is a small, private, liberal arts college in the Midwest. The college brought together students to participate in a 3-hour structured conversation/dialogue on racial literacy. The purpose of the dialogue was to create a campus-wide dialogue to better understand how to support a more inclusive campus—for students from historically marginalized groups in particular. I (Roger) designed this experience to have individuals engage in processes designed to support their personal development. This includes developing racial literacy, creating greater understanding of the importance of identity and identity development, creating greater understanding of the needs of marginalized students, defining concrete steps all can take to demonstrate allyship, and encouraging the development of the competencies needed to move forward in a growth-minded manner.

Contextual Influences

The following were relevant to consider prior to developing the curriculum for this dialogue:

Yourself, the Educator

My social identities as Latinx, as the child of immigrants, and as an individual whose family was on the receiving end of prejudicial experiences growing up were key influences into how I approached the creation of this workshop. I also leaned on the experiences

I had in my many years of leading these types of discussions and workshops in a variety of settings.

My deep familiarity with this campus community allowed me to recognize other factors that highlighted realities needing attention. For example, the campus has a growing population of students of color. The latest data showed that nearly 30% of students identified as students of color. In contrast, the teaching and administrative staff was over 90% White. This was an important factor that informed the need to include workshop components that focused on understanding cultural salience, history, implicit bias, and visible allyship.

This effort was a fairly new experience in the history of the institution. In my facilitation, I was mindful of how students might be experiencing the activities and the information being shared. I wanted to be sure to minimize the likelihood of retraumatizing students who may have had a difficult experience. My personal experience as a member of an underrepresented ethnic community was always on the forefront of my mind as I paid close attention to how underrepresented students were experiencing the workshop and the dialogue. I made sure to allow participants the space to create and set up explicit ground rules that would help guide our time together.

Student Influences

The majority of student participants largely came from a variety of student organizations, including students from cultural identity groups, student government, and resident assistants. Students came to this workshop from a variety of experiences. Some were deeply involved in the campus's diversity efforts. Some came to this workshop with little to no experience on these issues. The campus lacked a history of providing common trainings, and this experience was new to the community. Some students had experience or exposure to these issues through involvement on campus or through course work at SLAC. All were drawn to this workshop out of a desire to learn more, grow more in understanding of these issues, and help create a more connected and supportive campus community. On a campus that historically seemed apathetic to these issues, where attention to these issues usually arose only after a crisis, and where the institutional leadership often saw these issues as an afterthought, a program like this was an important step in disrupting the norms of the campus, imagining new paradigms, and developing a new ethos.

Environmental Influences

The students who chose to participate in this optional dialogue were motivated by a couple of factors. First, there was a sense of urgency around this work in the immediate aftermath of a racial incident that had occurred recently on campus. The incident involved a student on social media using a racial slur directed toward the campus community's students of color. The students of the community reacted swiftly and expressed outrage on social media. Their outrage was further fueled by the sense among students that the institution had not reacted quickly enough and did not communicate effectively the ways they were handling this situation.

Second, this most recent incident was another in a long history of incidents in which students of color had tried, with little success, to call attention to their experiences of being marginalized and minoritized. Because the campus had a reputation among students for being apathetic to these issues, students felt determined to "no longer be ignored" as the incident unfolded in real time and afterward.

As mentioned earlier, this dialogue was part of a larger effort to more intentionally engage the campus community in dialogue and to help inform the direction of SLAC's diversity, equity, and inclusion initiatives and work. The structured dialogue was designed to last 3 hours in order to create the time needed to build relationships, trust, a safe space for honest dialogue, and the background information to provide a foundational framework and context to understand issues of marginalization and the experiences of underrepresented students. It was a chance to dialogue about allyship and specific actions that could be taken to be more inclusive in our language, behavior, and actions. It was an opportunity to have students feel heard, seen, and appreciated.

Another important note to add is that this structured dialogue, while rooted in response to an incident, was an important step in making the case to provide more educational workshops for students to support their development in a proactive way. It was the recognition that educators have a responsibility to educate and lay the foundation for students to move forward in their own development on these issues. It was in the best interest of the institution to prepare its students for the interdependent, intercultural world they would enter after college.

Theories and Conceptual Frameworks

I used the MOD framework for this dialogue. So many of the issues that dominate the culture of inequity are rooted in a populace that is uniformed and lacks context to connect the dots between history and social inequity. This model helps provide a framework to get participants to think of these issues from a systemic perspective rather than as examples of individual behaviors. Understanding how systems of oppression work, how cultural salience is rooted in large part to the shared experiences of oppression, and how dominant groups gain advantage over others in these systems is necessary to create breakthroughs of awareness and consciousness. This framework was especially relevant in the divided campus response to the aforementioned racial incident. While underrepresented students felt hurt, unsupported, and unheard, a good majority of White students felt the students' and institution's reaction to the incident was overblown. The juxtaposition of these responses among students required a framework that could provide a common conceptual understanding and language to understand one another, and the impact of these incidents on their peers was a classic example of how greater privilege often leads to less empathy for others.

I-MMDI brought to light the lived experiences of people of color across a multitude of identities. While the dialogue was focused on racial literacy, the attention to intersections with other oppressed identities (e.g., sexuality, religion, gender, social class) helped bring to light how we carry multiple identities at all times and that systems of oppression have synergistic negative effects that are much more complex, impactful, and generational. In this experience, particular attention was given to students of color and their experience following the racial incident and their experiences overall as community members.

Cultural Consciousness and Learning Outcomes

The dialogue was an opportunity to engage the campus in an experience that would bring to light much of the anecdotal feedback the campus had received from students of color. It was also an opportunity to hear more direct experiences that painted a fuller picture of the campus climate data that had been collected over the last few years. Therefore, the primary content for the experience was focused on racially based knowledge at the cultural and community levels, as well as behaviors at the cultural or community levels. This focus on learning led to the adoption of three learning outcomes:

Students who participate in the racial literacy dialogue will do the following:

1. Define core concepts related to *social identity*, *salience*, and *privilege*.
2. Describe how historical and contemporary racial inequality influence the experience of racial communities.
3. Identify at least one personal behavior that challenges racial inequality.

This work will reach students in order to create deeper understanding of their own community and also provide a framework for engaging in their own "inner work" throughout their lifetime. This is crucial to connecting with the mission of SLAC, which includes preparation for a life of contribution and to practice cultural humility in their own growth and development on these issues. In an interdependent and global economy, every industry and professional field requires individuals who demonstrate the skill to confidently navigate diverse ideas, perspectives, and ways of being.

Pedagogical Considerations and Activities

The dialogue began with formal introductions and the setting up of ground rules. I had the participants collectively put together a set of ground rules for the dialogue. I asked, "What rules can we set and commit to that will allow us to listen to one another, respect one another, understand one another, and build community with one another?" Upon the setting of the rules, I took a few minutes to share an overview of our goals for our time together and any additional ground rules the group may not have considered. I explained that the 3 hours will have us engage in a variety of ways, all designed to build on one another.

The first 30 minutes involved multiple activities designed to lay the context—understanding cultural salience. I began with a mini lecture that involved a couple of slides: the "diversity iceberg" and the "blindfolded people and the elephant" (see Figure 9.1). In these examples, I engaged with participants to understand the meaning behind invisible and more readily visible aspects of diversity. I explained that even with "visible" aspects of diversity, we must check our assumptions because our own social lenses may inaccurately perceive and respond in ways that are harmful.

FIGURE 9.1. Image of blindfolded people and the elephant.

This led us to understanding salience, and here I distributed a handout that look at the varying spheres of our identities. I led students through a sequenced reflection activity with small group discussion activities in order to explore the ways identity influences their lives. I asked students to identify which of these 10 identities has the most meaning and significance for them and why. The 10 identities included race, ethnicity, gender/gender identity, sexual orientation, age, socioeconomic status, nationality, ability, religion, and immigrant status.

Once they completed this handout, they then reported how they responded in their small groups. I was mindful of how marginalized communities may have been impacted in these moments and always make sure that we adhered to the ground rule of "opting out" if an individual was triggered during this activity. By offering the option to opt out, I encouraged students to do whatever they need to do to take care of themselves, including stepping out. I asked them to feel free to not personally share but be attentive and supportive and an active listener for others.

I then asked students to review the 10 social identities they started with and reduce them to four social identities they felt were most salient to them. After another round of small group discussion, I had them reduce the number to one. After each round of reductions, I asked students to describe how easy or difficult is was to reduce their social identities. We reflected on the reality that, as human beings, we tend to hold on to and value most the social identities that are most dear to us and most present in our lived experiences in the world. This did not mean that the social identities that we had "let go of" in this activity were not valuable to us. Indeed, under different circumstances and different times in our lives, we may choose different social identities that are more salient. However, as a general rule, the social identity we find most salient, when asked to reduce the number to one, is the one we feel captures who we are at our core. To ensure time was allotted for deep conversation and insights, the entire sequence of reflection activities coupled with small group discussions took approximately 30 to 40 minutes to complete.

When we completed the activity, I led a large group discussion activity where I asked them what takeaways they had. I made sure to include understanding that salience matters, that we each walk through the world differently, that what is least salient often implies great privilege in that identity, and that structural inequities often enhance the identities in which we feel most salient and connected.

At the 45-minute mark I did a brief check-in and asked how students were feeling. I then reminded them of the ground rules we created and let them know that the next hour would be a difficult journey through America's racial history. In this portion of the dialogue, I put together a lecture about the racial history of the United States from 1600 to the present. Some eras on the history timeline received more time than others, but the point of the next hour was to awaken students to history that is typically little known. This history was important to cover because it created the foundation for understanding systemic oppression. I completed the hour with a simulation activity, a privilege walk. In this walk, I had the group run through varying scenarios that demonstrated the impact of power and privilege in our society.

I then followed the privilege walk with a few discussion-based activities. I took 20 minutes to debrief the experience as a large group. Upon completion of the debriefing, the participants were broken up into equal-sized small groups and asked to take 20 minutes to discuss questions related to how power and privilege have affected their lives. They were each asked to take a turn and share a time when they were victims of discrimination. After each participant and each group done (they were given a predetermined amount of time to complete it), they were asked to repeat the same process, this time talking about a time they discriminated against someone else.

I took the final 20 minutes to offer a mini lecture about best practices for creating culturally responsive schools and practicing cultural humility. I reminded students about cultural salience and that we are always on the journey for greater equity. I then allowed a few moments for all participants to share one word that captured their experience or how they felt after the dialogue.

The dialogue concluded with a reminder that we were all a work in progress.

Assessing Student Learning

The racial literacy dialogue was not directly assessed at the conclusion of the dialogue. However, given that the dialogue was intended to inform the development of

TABLE 9.1. Rubric for Racial Literacy Dialogue

	Below Expectations	*Meets Expectations*	*Exceeds Expectations*
Knowledge of Racial Inequality	Student does not identify at least two accurate examples of racial inequality	Student identifies at least two accurate examples of racial inequality *and* these examples are rooted in either the past *or* the present	Student identifies at least two accurate examples of racial inequality *and* these examples are rooted in both the past *and* the present
Impact of Racial Inequality on Racial Groups	Student does not accurately describe the impact of racial inequality on any racial groups *or* discuss the impact on racial groups generically	Student accurately describes the impact of racial inequality on at least *one* specifically named racial group	Student accurately describes the impact of racial inequality on at least *two* specifically named racial groups *or* describes the impact of racial inequality on the relationships between *two* specifically named racial groups
Knowledge of Personal Behaviors to Challenge Racial Inequality	Student does not identify any behaviors relevant to stopping racial inequality	Student identifies at least one behavior relevant to stopping racial inequality that is either *generic* or not related to themselves	Student identifies at least one behavior relevant to stopping racial inequality that is *specific* and related to themselves

future educational programs for students on campus, assessing the second and third learning outcomes would be most useful to identify gaps in student learning that might need to be more immediately addressed. If these outcomes were to be assessed, data would be needed from students who participated in the dialogue related to (a) their understanding of racial inequality, (b) how it influences the experiences of racial groups, and (c) a personal behavior to challenge racial inequality and its influence on racial groups. Collecting this information would require a prompt; however, data might need to be collected from students after the dialogue had ended. Specifically, an electronic survey could be distributed to students asking them to complete the survey within two weeks to be entered into a raffle to win a $20 gift certificate to the campus bookstore to motivate their participation. The survey could have a single, open-ended question, such as the following:

After having participated in this week's racial literacy dialogue, please take a moment to think about what you have learned from this experience. In at least 150 words, please reflect on your understanding about racial inequality and your commitment to address racial inequality on our campus. Specifically, (a) describe at least two specific ways racial inequality exists, (b) describe how the presence of racial inequality impacts oppressed racial groups, and (c) name at least one behavior you can do to stop racial inequality on campus.

Data could then be analyzed using a rubric with three domains: two domains associated with the second learning outcome and one domain associated with the third learning outcome (see Table 9.1). Successful learning would be achieved if students meet or exceeded expectations for each domain.

Handout 9.1
Reflecting on Contextual Influences:
Yourself, the Educator

1. Identify your social identities and circle those that you believe are most salient to this workshop or structured conversation.

   a. Race: **White-Brown**
   b. Ethnicity: **Hispanic-Latinx**
   c. Sex: **Male**
   d. Gender: **Cisgender man**
   e. Sexual orientation: **Heterosexual**
   f. Ability status: **Able-bodied**
   g. Religion or faith: **None**
   h. Social class: **Raised working class; currently middle class**
   i. Other: **Child of immigrants**
   j. Other:

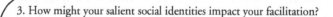

2. How do you enact your most salient social identities?

As a Latinx son of immigrants, I draw on my personal experiences related to race and ethnicity when planning the curriculum for this structured conversation on race. My racial identity as a White-passing Brown man also shapes how I view myself in relationship to this topic. While my children view me as Brown, in many other circles I am perceived as White. My collective experiences shape how I enter conversations on race and ethnicity with extra attention to how I am perceived by others.

3. How might your salient social identities impact your facilitation?

These social identities impact my ability to connect with underrepresented folks who may have had similar experiences of marginalization. However, I am also aware of the privilege I carry and the responsibility I feel to not speak from a place of authority in regard to social identities I do not carry. I must remind myself to speak from a place of allyship, solidarity, and humility.

Reflecting on Contextual Influences:
Student and Environmental Influences

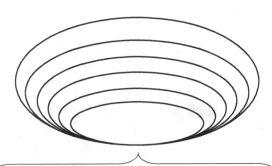

When considering student influences:

4. What *demographics* are present among the students that might be most relevant to the workshop or structured conversation?

Students of color make-up approximately 30% of the student body on campus. However, students of color are most likely to attend the dialogue.

5. What prior *knowledge* or relevant formal or informal education experiences have these students shared prior to this workshop or structured conversation, and how might that shape how different students engage the experience?

Students who are most likely to attend will have engaged in a variety of on-campus programs. Due to the history of the institution and its lack of attention on racial issues, students will likely view this dialogue as a great leap forward.

6. What might *motivate* different students to attend or fully participate in this workshop or structured conversation, and how might that shape the nature of their participation?

Students will be motivated to participate by their desire to learn more and contribute to a supportive campus community that will benefit all students, including themselves.

When considering environmental influences:

7. How might *educational* factors, including prior content covered, existing group dynamics, and the duration of the experience, shape the workshop or structured conversation?

The 3-hour session will allow for the formation of a very basic foundation from which to move forward. However, momentum gained from this experience can benefit future efforts to offer more racial dialogues on campus to reach more students.

8. What recent *campus* events or potential campus climate concerns might different students have that are relevant to how they perceive or experience the workshop or structured conversation?

Recent incidents of racial slurs on social media have fueled the desire for real and substantive community-building events and educational offerings on race and inclusion.

9. What relevant recent *off-campus* issues at the local, state, or national levels might influence different students' perceptions of or experience during the workshop or structured conversation?

Nationally, the rise of White supremacy and affiliated groups, along with the long history of police brutality toward people of color, are at the forefront of students' consciousness. These issues are exacerbated when racial bias incidents occur on campus.

Handout 9.2
Reflecting on Theories and Conceptual Frameworks
Relative to Contextual Influences

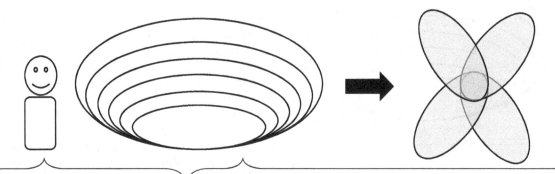

1. Which theories or frameworks resonate the most with you and your approach to social justice education?

Matrix of domination

2. How might your social identities and related experiences influence the theories or conceptual frameworks that you default to using in this work?

My racial experiences in my personal life and on college campuses strongly shapes my desire for others to understand how racial privilege and oppression exist in society as described by the matrix of domination.

3. Which theories or conceptual frameworks seem useful given what you know about the students, specifically related to the following:

a. Demographics

Intersectional model of multiple dimensions of identity

b. Prior knowledge

Matrix of domination

c. Motivation to participate

Intersectional model of multiple dimensions of identity

4. Which theories or conceptual frameworks seem useful given the environment, specifically related to the following:

a. Expectations from stakeholders for the workshop or structured conversation

Matrix of domination

b. Amount of time you have for the workshop or structured conversation

Matrix of domination

c. Relevant issues on campus or from the broader social environment that may be pressing on students

Matrix of domination

Handout 9.3
Reflecting on Cultural Consciousness Content Areas and Learning Outcomes

1. Using the matrix of cultural consciousness to the right, place an "x" in the squares to indicate which content areas are most essential for this learning experience.

2. Why are these content areas most essential?

This dialogue needs to promote understanding about racialized experiences in the world generally and specifically to different social identity groups related to race. Therefore, the focus for the dialogue should be on knowledge and behaviors to promote further understanding and exploration about race.

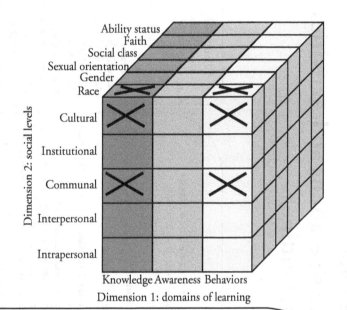

3. For each content area identified, transform it into a single learning outcome statement. For each learning outcome statement, ensure it includes all three parts and satisfies the seven best practices for writing learning outcomes:

_____**Students**_____ who _____**participate in the racial literacy dialogue**_____
        (Audience)   (Condition)

will be able to:

Behavior a. **Define core concepts related to *social identity*, *salience*, and *privilege***

Behavior b. **Describe how historical and contemporary racial inequality influence the experience of racial communities**

Behavior c. **Identify at least one personal behavior that challenges racial inequality**

Behavior checklist:
- ✓ Meaningful
- ✓ Tied to learning
- ✓ Uses action verbs
- ✓ Observable
- ✓ Measurable
- ✓ Written at an appropriate level
- ✓ Clear and concise

Handout 9.4

Reflecting on Pedagogical Considerations and Activities
(Building an Outline)

1. List your learning outcomes.

a. Define core concepts related to *social identity*, *salience*, and *privilege* (addressed by activities b–d, f, g)

b. Describe how historical and contemporary racial inequality influence the experience of racial communities (addressed by activities d–g)

c. Identify at least one personal behavior that challenges racial inequality (addressed by activity h)

2. Create an outline for your workshop or structured conversation that identifies specific activities and approximate time durations. Also note discussion questions for discussion-based activities.

a. Guidelines for conversation (10 minutes)

b. Lecture activity: Defining *salience* (10 minutes)

c. Introspective activity with small group discussion: Salience (40 minutes)
 - What was this activity like for you?
 - Which social identities do you identify with most and least?
 - How do you express your social identities in your daily life?
 - How do your social identities intersect in your daily life?
 - What do you wish others knew about you and any of your identities?

d. Lecture activity: America's racial history (40 minutes)

e. Simulation activity: Privilege walk (10 minutes)

f. Large group discussion (20 minutes)
 - How did you feel during the activity and why?
 - What statements resonated with you an why?
 - How has privilege affected your life?

g. Small group discussion (20 minutes)
 - Share a time when you were a victim of discrimination.
 - Share a time when you discriminated against someone else.

h. Lecture activity: Imagining cultural responsiveness (20 minutes)

Five principles

#1: Facilitate the development of knowledge, awareness, and behaviors (addressed by activities b–h)

#2: Utilize students' knowledge and experiences (addressed by activities b, c, e–g)

#3: Help students understand their positionality within systems of inequality (addressed by activities c, e–g)

#4: Engage emotional and cognitive aspects of learning (addressed by activities b, c, e–g)

#5: Establish a welcoming and inclusive environment (addressed by activity a)

3. State which activities address both (a) the learning outcomes on the left and (b) the principles on the right. Modify your outline until it addresses all of your learning outcomes and principles for social justice education

Handout 9.5
Reflecting on Assessing Student Learning

Think about each step in the assessment process and draft your plan:

1. What learning outcomes will be assessed?

   Describe how historical and contemporary racial inequality influence the experience of racial communities.

   Identify at least one personal behavior that challenges racial inequality.

2. Given your learning outcomes, what data do you need, and from whom?

   Data needed:

   a. Students' understanding of racial inequality

   b. Students' understanding of how racial inequality influences specific racial groups

   c. Students' ability to identify personal behaviors that challenge racial inequality

   Data collected from:

   Students who participated in the dialogue

3. What tools are needed to collect and analyze data? Check each tool you need and state which types of data on the left will be collected from each tool you plan to use.

   □ Learning survey

   ✓ **Writing prompt (a, b, c)**
   (Delivered via an electronic survey)

   ✓ **Rubric**

4a. When will you collect your data?

   □ During the experience

   □ At the end of the experience

   ✓ **After the experience**

   ✓ When: **The next day**

4b. How will you incentivize data collection?

   Raffle for a $20 gift certificate for the campus bookstore

5a. When analyzing your data, what will be your threshold for success?

   Students must meet or exceed expectations for all domains of the rubric.

5b. When will you make time to analyze and interpret your data to improve the experience?

   After the end of the term

Handout 9.6
Circles of Salience

PLEASE WRITE YOUR FIRST NAME IN THE MIDDLE CIRCLE
AND AWAIT FURTHER INSTRUCTIONS.

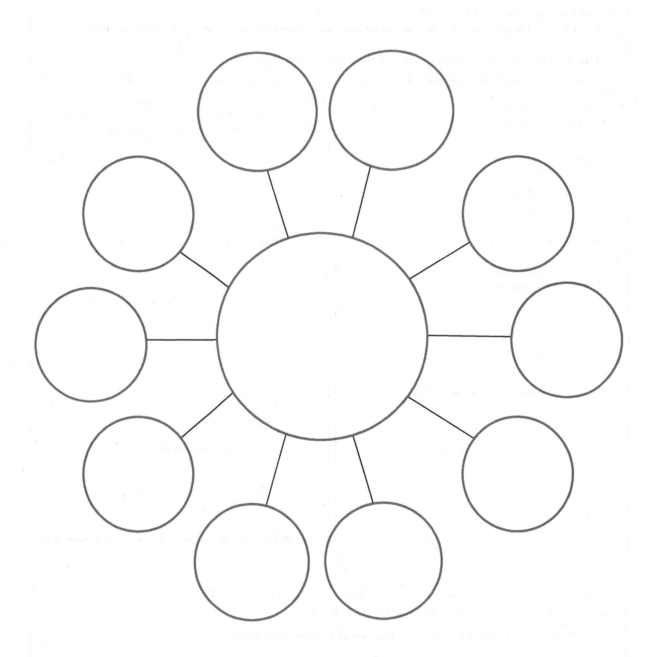

CHAPTER 10

Social Inequality Workshop for Regional Teacher Nonprofit (RTN)

Regional Teacher Nonprofit (RTN) is a large state-based organization that awards approximately 100 scholarships to high school graduates pursuing degrees in K–12 education. The organization expected students to complete a summer-long training experience as a condition of their scholarship after their first year in college. Part of the training experience included a single 2-hour training to discuss issues of social inequality in general and related to their future careers in K–12 education. RTN staff asked for the training to focus on building knowledge about social inequality and increasing students' awareness of inequality in their future careers. I (Scott) designed the workshop curriculum for me, with support from RNT's paraprofessional staff, to facilitate small group activities as needed.

Contextual Influences

The following were relevant to consider prior to developing the curriculum for this workshop:

Yourself, the Educator

My social identities as a White, cisgender man and related experiences as a higher education professional influenced my approach to this session. At the time of this workshop, I worked as the head of a department that advocated for program and policy changes to serve minoritized student communities on campus. Doing this work within my privileged positionality provided much insight into the power and responsibility educators have over the day-to-day student experience. While I was more readily able to identify and advocate

on race and cisgender issues, I was relatively slower to identify and acknowledge issues faced by students who identified as transgender. Therefore, I developed a practice to reflect on my social identities to minimize my blind spots and be intentional about having conversations with students to inform my advocacy efforts on their behalf.

These professional experiences as an educator and my associated reflective processes heightened my awareness of race and gender within this workshop. When facilitating, I was extra attentive when students of color, cisgender women, and transgender students wanted to participate in the session to ensure they had space to give voice to their experiences. Additionally, when lecturing on the educational context, I used personal examples related to race and gender to highlight my own areas of growth and demonstrate practices to help mitigate how my privilege intersects with my positional authority as an educator.

Student Influences

This training on social inequality impacted approximately 100 rising sophomore college students majoring in K–12 education from various colleges and universities across one state located in the Midwest. RTN did not collect demographic data on these students; however, the majority of these students were White, cisgender female and from urban or suburban communities. These students did not share common coursework or experiences because they came from different colleges and universities across the state.

Students' prior knowledge was informed by their individual educational and social experiences on their respective campuses. RTN's staff assumed these students had no prior content knowledge related to social inequality or its application to K–12 education. However, because all of these students were majoring in K–12 education, a fair assumption was that these students had some level of interest in educational systems and could draw on their own experiences as students themselves. Last, the broader RTN training curriculum did explicitly talk about race and social class with these students throughout the summer.

The placement of this workshop within the required summer training influenced students' motivation to participate in the experience. In order to continue receiving their college scholarship, students had to attend the entire summer training experience.

Environmental Influences

While this workshop occurred as part of the broader summer training, it did not build on previous content. Because this was a training, there were no expectations of students to prepare for these sessions, eliminating the possibility of assigning readings or online modules to complete prior to the workshop. However, the 2-hour window was ample time to provide foundation knowledge and additional application.

The summer training used a mixture of large and small group time every day. Large group sessions introduced content to the students. RTN staff led small group sessions with approximately 20 students each to facilitate reflection that was more personal and able to directly apply to the students' teaching roles (e.g., elementary education, high school science). The oscillating structure of the summer training made it likely that students had familiarity with many students in the entire group and had stronger relationships among students in their small groups. Additionally, students likely had some relationships with other students who may have also attended the same college or university. These existing relationships and the common focus on K–12 education helped facilitate deeper reflection among these students.

Student interaction with the campus environment was largely irrelevant since this training happened off campus over the summer. However, any incidents or challenging issues that could have occurred during the summer training would have been very relevant to developing the workshop had they arisen. Nationally, there were multiple, highly relevant issues to K–12 education that these students were likely aware of and

thinking about in some fashion. These included the It Gets Better Project, the Black Lives Matter movement, the #MeToo movement, and attention to policies and practices related to transgender students' use of locker rooms and bathrooms.

Theories and Conceptual Frameworks

While I prefer SIDM as an educator, the workshop focus requested from RTN, coupled with the contextual influences identified, called for the use of frameworks that focus on systemic understanding across a range of social identities. The MOD framework was well suited to frame the conversation about social inequality in the world and institutions of education. Additionally, I-MMDI was helpful for students to contextualize social inequality in their own lives across multiple social identities they hold.

The MOD framework was valuable given the desire for the workshop to focus primarily on social inequality and the fact that students' primary identity would be that of future educators within K–12 institutions. Additionally, the broader social issues related to race, gender, and sexuality were relevant and timely topics for K–12 education, topics that these students will be thinking about in their training. I-MMDI was useful to help students feel personally connected to issues of social inequality and the ways in which they replicate and experience harm by these systems. These frameworks together were useful to tap into students' prior knowledge about social inequality in their own K–12 education experiences. Last, the expectation of RTN to focus on both knowledge and awareness of social inequality supported the decision to use both frameworks, and a 2-hour workshop provided ample time to address both in meaningful ways.

Cultural Consciousness and Learning Outcomes

A 2-hour workshop provided enough time to examine multiple content areas. Because RTN requested the workshop focus specifically on the knowledge and awareness domains of learning, it was possible to explore a wider range of social levels and social identities. Specifically, the desire to examine the presence and operation of social inequality as a fact lent itself to focus on knowledge at the cultural, institutional, and interpersonal levels related to race, gender, and sexual orientation given the contextual influences previously identified. Additionally, the desire to cultivate personal awareness of social inequality as future educators lent itself to cultivate awareness at the cultural, institutional, interpersonal, and intrapersonal levels across multiple social identities based on those identities most salient to the students themselves. Collectively, these content areas allowed students to learn about social inequality in the world while applying that knowledge to themselves through their personal experiences and professional aspirations as educators.

This focus for the workshops funneled into four primary learning outcomes that explicitly tend to the knowledge and awareness at the cultural, institutional, and interpersonal levels:

Scholarship students who participate in the training workshop will be able to do the following:

1. Define concepts of *privilege, oppression* and *social inequality.*
2. Articulate how inequality is manifested in society and in schools.
3. Articulate different causes of inequality in society and in schools.
4. Identify personal attitudes and behaviors that contribute to inequality.

The first learning outcome attended to the knowledge and awareness domains at the cultural level. The second and third learning outcomes attended to the knowledge and awareness domains, but focused on the K–12 educator at the institutional levels. The fourth learning outcome again attended to the knowledge domain at the interpersonal level and the awareness domain at the interpersonal and intrapersonal levels. Because all of these outcomes were achievable through the cultivation of both knowledge and awareness, it was important to recognize the different approaches used for each that transcend the specific learning outcomes. The knowledge domain was examined specific to race, gender, and sexuality through the choice of examples; however, the awareness domain did not center on specific social identities so that students could cultivate awareness through their most salient social identities. Looking at the third learning outcome as an example, the workshop taught students about the causes of

inequality with specific examples related to race, gender, and sexual orientation. However, the facilitators could invite students to apply their knowledge about the causes of inequality through any social identity.

These learning outcomes satisfied the expectations of well-written outcome statements. The outcomes were meaningful for RTN and their students who would work in K–12 education. The first and fourth outcomes were written at a simpler level that is appropriate to ensure students obtained basic knowledge and awareness. The second and third outcomes were written at an intermediate level that reasonably expects students to apply their knowledge and awareness in a society or educational context. All of these outcomes used actions verbs ("define," "identify," and "articulate") that required students to use their own words to directly demonstrate learning in an observable and measurable way. While these outcomes may seem somewhat vague, they allowed sufficient room for students to demonstrate knowledge and awareness in multiple ways given their social identities and future role in the field of K–12 education.

Pedagogical Considerations and Activities

A single 2-hour curriculum used six activities to achieve all four learning outcomes. After general introductions, the first 5-minute activity involved reviewing a prefabricated list of guidelines for conversation that students were asked to review, modify if desired, and agree to for the remainder of the workshop. Second was a 15-minute lecture that defined the concepts of *privilege, oppression,* and *social inequality;* explained how these concepts relate to one another; and stated how these concepts are manifested in society overall and during interpersonal interactions. Third was a 15-minute simulation activity regarding social inequality. This activity involved distributing playing cards to all students, having the students display their cards so that they could not see their own card, and instructing them to treat one another based on the perceived value of the playing card. The first, second, and third activities all happened in the large group format.

The fourth activity involved breaking students into small groups for a 40-minute small-group discussion led by a RTN staff member. Students were broken into the same small groups they had been using for other purposes for the summer training to build on previous relationships and maximize conversation. Discussion questions focused on the way students felt and what they observed during the simulation. Additional discussion questions invited students to apply their experience during the simulation to their personal lives; to the concepts of privilege, oppression, and social inequality; and to their future roles as educators.

After these small group discussions finished, all groups returned to a large group format for the final activities of the training. The fifth activity involved a 20-minute large group discussion that focused on recapping highlights from the small group discussion and further exploring the ways educators create or replicate social inequality in their roles in K–12 education. Sixth was a lecture activity that explored how social inequality is created and maintained in K–12 education overall and during teacher-student interactions. The curriculum paid specific attention to how social inequality manifests itself through language, practice, and policies within classrooms or schools overall. The workshop ended by reviewing key takeaways and providing ways students could continue to examine their relationship to social inequality in K–12 education.

This curriculum addressed all five principles for social justice education. Students developed their knowledge and awareness through all activities except the guidelines for conversation. Behaviors were not an intentional focus of the training; however, the discussion-based activities provided opportunities to practice key behaviors related to critically examining and discussing social inequality. Students' prior knowledge and experiences were actively cultivated in two ways: through the creation of a shared experience via the simulation activity and by inviting students to apply what felt familiar to them from the simulation to their own lives. Relatedly, these same activities intentionally engaged students' thoughts and feelings through the simulation and purposeful discussion questions that examined what they felt and noticed. Students explored their positionality through the small and large group discussion activities and through the lecture activity that examined social inequality specific to teachers in K–12 education. Last, attempts to establish an inclusive and welcoming learning environment occurred by timing the training to happen a few weeks into the summer training, using existing small groups for discussion, and establishing guidelines for discussion at the start of the training.

Assessing Student Learning

At the time of this partnership, RTN did not implement a plan to assess student learning for the training. However, if RTN was interested in assessing student learning, they could have implemented the following approach. Among the four learning outcomes identified, the second and third outcomes were most relevant to the immediate needs of RTN to prepare students for their future careers in K–12 education. These two learning outcomes required data to be collected from students about their understanding of how inequality was manifested and caused in both society at large and schools in particular. Because there was a wide range of possible responses related to their personal experiences, a writing prompt and rubric collected and analyzed students' data. The following writing prompt was distributed to students at the end of the workshop and collected before the end of the summer training as a stipulation of their scholarship:

> In one to two pages, explicitly reflect on the nature of social inequality, in terms of either privilege or oppression, in the context of society overall, K–12 schools, and your personal life. Specifically identify at least two examples of social inequality, one example that exists in society overall and one different example that exists in the K–12 school setting. For both examples, explicitly (a) describe the example of social inequality and which social identity groups it impacts, (b) explain what makes it an example of social inequality in terms of privilege or oppression, and (c) explain what contributed to the cause of such social inequality. Your response should reflect an accurate understanding of social inequality using at least two concrete examples.

Based on this prompt, an internally created rubric with four domains that corresponded to the manifestation and cause of social inequality in both the societal and K–12 context (see Table 10.1) could be used to analyze student responses. Successful student learning would be achieved if students met or exceeded expectations in each domain.

TABLE 10.1. Potential Rubric for Training

		Below Expectations	*Meets Expectations*	*Exceeds Expectations*
Societal Context	*Manifestation of Social Inequality*	Student does not provide an accurate example of social inequality linked to a specific social identity group	Student provides an accurate example of social inequality that explicitly addresses *either* privilege or oppression linked to a specific social identity group	Student provides an accurate example of social inequality that explicitly addresses *both* privilege and oppression linked to specific social identity groups
	Cause of Social Inequality	Student does not provide an accurate cause of social inequality	Student provides an accurate cause of social inequality associated at an *individual* level	Student provides an accurate cause of social inequality associated at an *institutional* level
K–12 Context	*Manifestation of Social Inequality*	Student does not provide an accurate example of social inequality	Student provides an accurate example of social inequality that explicitly addresses *either* privilege or oppression linked to a specific social identity group	Student provides an accurate example of social inequality that explicitly addresses *both* privilege and oppression linked to specific social identity groups
	Cause of Social Inequality	Student does not provide an accurate cause of social inequality	Student provides an accurate cause of social inequality associated at an *individual* level	Student provides an accurate cause of social inequality associated at an *institutional* level

Handout 10.1
Reflecting on Contextual Influences:
Yourself, the Educator

1. Identify your social identities and circle those that you believe are most salient to this workshop or structured conversation.

a.	Race:	**White**
b.	Ethnicity:	**German**
c.	Sex:	**Male**
d.	Gender:	**Cisgender man**
e.	Sexual orientation:	**Heterosexual**
f.	Ability status:	**Able-bodied**
g.	Religion or faith:	**Non-Christian**
h.	Social class:	**Raised working class; currently middle class**
i.	Other:	
j.	Other:	

2. How do you enact your most salient social identities?

Having a heightened awareness of my social identities related to race and gender attunes me to the race and gender dynamics in the workshop. I am increasingly conscious of how cisgender women, transgender students, and students of color participate in the session and make extra attempts to bring their voice into the experience and ensure their experiences are represented in the session. Because I inherit privilege related to both my race and gender social identities, I explicitly discuss how my privileged social identities influence what I think, believe, and do in the session as a model for how others can engage in self-reflection. Additionally, I model vulnerability by explicitly verbalizing what I do not know, stating what is beyond my experience, and thanking students when they point out my blind spots.

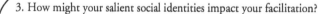

3. How might your salient social identities impact your facilitation?

I intentionally use my racial and gendered experiences in my career as part of my facilitation practice. I explicitly verbalize my internal thoughts and reflective practices about my race and gender to show students how I approach this self-work to simultaneously facilitate the session and model facilitation from my positionality with privilege.

Reflecting on Contextual Influences: Student and Environmental Influences

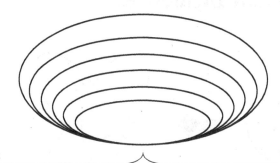

When considering student influences:

4. What *demographics* are present among the students that might be most relevant to the workshop or structured conversation?

There are approximately 100 rising sophomore college students who will be in this workshop. Specific data is not collected on these students. However, students are primarily White, female, and from urban or suburban areas.

5. What prior *knowledge* or relevant formal or informal education experiences have these students shared prior to this workshop or structured conversation, and how might that shape how different students engage the experience?

Students have no shared experiences related to diversity and social justice content. However, because they are all future K–12 educators, they have discussed teaching K–12 students with explicit attention to race and social class identities. They also have personal experiences as K–12 students themselves.

6. What might *motivate* different students to attend or fully participate in this workshop or structured conversation, and how might that shape the nature of their participation?

Students are required to participate in the session because it is embedded in their training they must complete as a condition for receiving their scholarship.

When considering environmental influences:

7. How might *educational* factors, including prior content covered, existing group dynamics, and the duration of the experience, shape the workshop or structured conversation?

The session lasts 2 hours and will not build on previous content. The session occurs 1 month into their summer training, so social dynamics will already be in place. Students are placed into small groups all summer for personal reflection and are likely spaces where students will have stronger existing relationships.

8. What recent *campus* events or potential campus climate concerns might different students have that are relevant to how they perceive or experience the workshop or structured conversation?

This summer training transcends local college campus experiences and is not relevant to this workshop.

9. What relevant recent *off-campus* issues at the local, state, or national levels might influence different students' perceptions of or experience during the workshop or structured conversation?

National issues relevant to K–12 education include the It Gets Better Project, the #MeToo movement, the Black Lives Matter movement, and transgender bathroom and locker room access.

Handout 10.2
Reflecting on Theories and Conceptual Frameworks
Relative to Contextual Influences

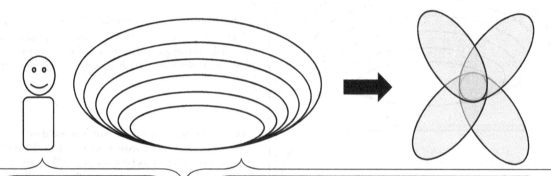

1. Which theories or frameworks resonate the most with you and your approach to social justice education?

Social identity development model

2. How might your social identities and related experiences influence the theories or conceptual frameworks that you default to using in this work?

My experience as an undergraduate student learning about my privilege through the lens of my oppressed social identities aligns with the developmental trajectory described by social identity development model.

3. Which theories or conceptual frameworks seem useful given what you know about the students, specifically related to the following:

a. Demographics

Matrix of domination

b. Prior knowledge

Matrix of domination; intersectional model of multiple dimensions of identity

c. Motivation to participate

Intersectional model of multiple dimensions of identity

4 Which theories or conceptual frameworks seem useful given the environment, specifically related to the following:

a. Expectations from stakeholders for the workshop or structured conversation

Matrix of domination; intersectional model of multiple dimensions of identity

b. Amount of time you have for the workshop or structured conversation

Matrix of domination; intersectional model of multiple dimensions of identity

c. Relevant issues on campus or from the broader social environment that may be pressing on students

Matrix of domination

Handout 10.3
Reflecting on Cultural Consciousness Content Areas and Learning Outcomes

1. Using the matrix of cultural consciousness to the right, place an "x" in the squares to indicate which content areas are most essential for this learning experience.

2. Why are these content areas most essential?

This training is the only time students will learn about social inequality in K–12 education. Therefore, the training should focus on how inequality operates and how students reinforce inequality in their professional roles.

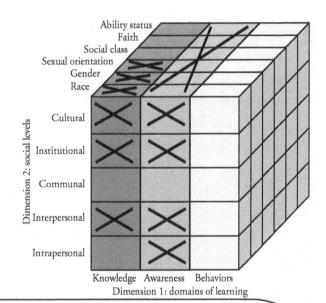

3. For each content area identified, transform it into a single learning outcome statement. For each learning outcome statement, ensure it includes all three parts and satisfies the seven best practices for writing learning outcomes:

<u>_____Scholarship students_____</u> who <u>_____participate in the training workshop_____</u>
             (Audience)   (Condition)

will be able to:

Behavior a. **Define concepts of *privilege*, *oppression*, and *social inequality***

Behavior b. **Articulate how inequality is manifested in society and in schools**

Behavior c. **Articulate different causes of inequality in society and in schools**

Behavior d. **Identify personal attitudes and behaviors that contribute to inequality**

Behavior checklist:
- ✓ Meaningful
- ✓ Tied to learning
- ✓ Uses action verbs
- ✓ Observable
- ✓ Measurable
- ✓ Written at an appropriate level
- ✓ Clear and concise

Handout 10.4
Reflecting on Pedagogical Considerations and Activities
(Building an Outline)

1. List your learning outcomes.

a. Define concepts of *privilege, oppression* and *social inequality* (addressed by activity b)

b. Articulate ways inequality is manifested in society and in schools (addressed by activities c–f)

c. Articulate different causes of inequality in society and in schools (addressed by activities d–f)

d. Identify personal attitudes and behaviors that contribute to inequality (addressed by activities c–e)

2. Create an outline for your workshop or structured conversation that identifies specific activities, approximate time durations, and specific discussion questions for discussion-based activities.

a. Guidelines for conversation activity (5 minutes)

b. Lecture activity: Social inequality (15 minutes)

c. Simulation activity: Social inequality (15 minutes)

d. Small group discussion (40 minutes)
  – How did you feel during the activity?
  – What did you notice during the activity?
  – What felt familiar about this activity?
  – What happened that relates to concepts of social inequality?
  – How do educators perpetuate social inequality?

e. Large group discussion (20 minutes)
  – How did the small group debriefs go?
  – What compelling themes did you notice and talk about?
  – How do educators perpetuate social inequality?

f. Lecture activity: Social inequality in education (15 minutes)

g. Takeaways and conclusion (5 minutes)

<u>Five Principles</u>

#1: Facilitate the development of knowledge, awareness, and behaviors **(addressed by activities b–f)**

#2: Utilize students' knowledge and experiences **(addressed by activities c–e)**

#3: Help students understand their positionality within systems of inequality **(addressed by activities d–f)**

#4: Engage emotional and cognitive aspects of learning **(addressed by activities c–e)**

#5: Establish a welcoming and inclusive environment **(addressed by activity a)**

3. State which activities address both (a) the learning outcomes on the left and (b) the principles on the right. Modify your outline until it addresses all of your learning outcomes and principles for social justice education

Handout 10.5
Reflecting on Assessing Student Learning

Think about each step in the assessment process and draft your plan:

1. What learning outcomes will be assessed?
   Articulate how inequality is manifested in society and in schools.
   Articulate different causes of inequality in society and in schools.

2. Given your learning outcomes, what data do you need, and from whom?

Data needed:

a. Students' understanding of how inequality is both manifested and caused in society

b. Students' understanding of how inequality is both manifested and caused in schools

Data collected from:

Students who participated in the training

3. What tools are needed to collect and analyze data? Check each tool you need and state which types of data on the left will be collected from each tool you plan to use.

   ☐ Learning survey

   ✓ **Writing prompt (a, b)**

   ✓ **Rubric**

4a. When will you collect your data?

   ☐ During the experience

   ☐ At the end of the experience

   ✓ **After the experience**

   When: **Before the end of summer**

4b. How will you incentivize data collection?

Required as part of completing the summer training

5a. When analyzing your data, what will be your threshold for success?
   Students must meet or exceed expectations for all domains of the rubric.

5b. When will you make time to analyze and interpret your data to improve the experience?
   After the end of the summer training

Handout 10.6
Social Inequality: The Pieces and Impact

Social inequality:
Refers to the unequal treatment, distribution of resources, and overall power among social groups based on their group identity

Social Privilege:
Benefits *received* by a person on the basis of who they are (their social identities), not what they have done or accomplished

Social Oppression:
Benefits *denied* to a person on the basis of who they are (their social identities), not what they have done or accomplished

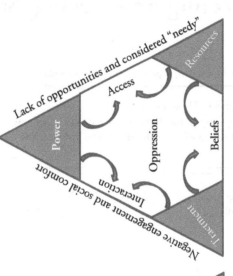

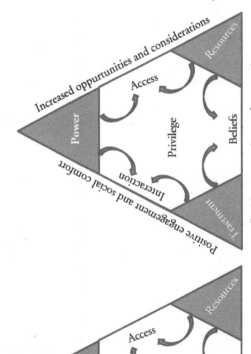

Conclusion: Ensuring Social Justice and Advancing Education

Looking ahead at the future of higher education, we believe that the need for deliberately designed and facilitated social justice education workshops and structured conversations will increase over time. As this need increases, institutions will rely on professionals, graduate students, and undergraduate peer educators to meet this growing demand. Therefore, it will be imperative that our community of social justice educators be prepared to help develop and facilitate these educational experiences. Make no mistake, our social justice education experiences are critical to educate our students to become better citizens in our communities and help lead our world toward a more socially just future. As such, we must ask ourselves: To what extent are we able to support the type of educational experiences that both our students and institutions need from us?

This book provides a path forward for newer professionals, graduate students, and peer educators to prepare themselves to intentionally design, facilitate, and assess social justice education experiences. Specifically, this book provides you with proven processes and frameworks to develop your own workshops and structured conversations to achieve your educational goals. After all, how successful is an educational experience that is not tailored to the facilitator and the students they will serve? Implementing an untailored educational experience would be similar to wearing someone else's outfit to a dance. While you might be dressed the right way on the outside, the outfit may not fit well enough to allow you to move as you wish, feel confident, or be your authentic self. In the case of social justice workshops and structured conversations, we believe that their effectiveness is limited if we fail to consider the context for learning, utilize scholarly frameworks, develop focused learning outcomes, select activities that adhere to social justice principles, require sufficient reflection prior to facilitation, and assess student learning to guide future improvement.

The first four chapters of this book outlined an intentional process to *design* social justice education workshops and structured conversations. We wrote each of these chapters to help you be mindful of a socially just process that is identity conscious, student centered, and pragmatic. This process is equally as important as the goal of creating the educational experience itself. Social justice education assumes students' social identities and related experiences matter and shape their needs, so it makes sense that this is the starting point for us when designing curricula. Additionally, we must remember that we ourselves are people with social identities and related experiences. Who we are and how we make sense of our experiences shapes our interpretation of the students we serve and influences the theoretical and conceptual frameworks we use to promote student development. Prepared with a clear sense of what students need and how to encourage their development, we can then identify and prioritize areas for learning and transform them into concrete learning outcomes. These outcomes, when shared with our students, help them be self-directed in their learning and true partners in their education. Finally, we should select activities to facilitate student learning and curate them to satisfy the educational principles of social justice education *after* we have thoughtfully considered the first three steps in this process.

In addition to providing a process to develop social justice education curricula, chapters 5 and 6 focused on *facilitating* and *assessing* curriculum to maximize student learning in the moment and in future iterations of the educational experience. These chapters remind us that the educational experience and associated activities are the front-facing part of our work. However, we as facilitators are the most powerful educational tool we have, and we have a duty to know ourselves and hone our skills to maximize our impact. Relatedly, assessment of student learning is equally necessary to know the actual impact of the educational experience in order to improve our efforts or identify what worked well for the future. In the current higher education climate, where data is becoming more essential in our work, we must be prepared to collect and analyze evidence to improve on, defend, and advocate on behalf of our work. While it is justifiable to be skeptical about assessment and cautious about reducing our work to numbers, such skepticism and caution ought not to prevent us from being empirically mindful and evidence based in our practice.

The proactive process we describe in this book has numerous benefits. Our educational experiences are more relevant and useful to students when we consider the context of our students and how we ourselves influence the education space we create and facilitate. We are more successful at promoting student development when we utilize theories and conceptual frameworks based on how students see themselves and the world around them, along with paths to enhance their understanding. Prioritizing student learning helps educators be purposeful in their efforts and better stewards of time, both their and their students' alike. Selecting activities to achieve the intended learning outcomes and adhere to social justice education principles ensures congruence between the intended and actual educational experience. Developing facilitation skills and reflecting on ourselves increases our capacity for engaging and responsive teaching. Assessing student learning ensures we can improve our educational experiences and build on our successes. Overall, taking the time to tailor our educational experiences to our students and ourselves is good for everyone.

The process described in this book is equally useful in reactive situations. Institutions routinely expect social justice educators to react to urgent student concerns or timely campus climate incidents. In these circumstances, it is even more important that social justice education experiences are designed using a purposeful process. When educators do not make time to tailor their approach, they might be tempted to seek out a "canned" curriculum designed for another student audience, rely on activities that were personally powerful without considering its relevance to their students, or simply "wing it" with a set of questions and "see what happens." While some educators might rationalize these methods, this book provides us with the insight and tools to be intentional in our processes

in both proactive and reactive situations. The nature of our work and reality of last-minute requests will not likely change soon, so we must find different ways to approach our work to ensure we give it the time and attention it requires for student learning to be both successful and socially just.

As you implement this process in your own practice, we would like to offer a final consideration to maximize the content we provide in this book. We designed this book for you to use every time you develop, facilitate, and assess a social justice education workshop or structured conversation. The text of each chapter presents and explains core ideas and poses central reflection questions for your consideration. However, the handouts at the end of each chapter are for you to make copies and complete. *We strongly encourage you to document your process.*

Documenting your process is a benefit to both yourself and the broader community of social justice educators. Documenting your process, including your assumptions and choices, is helpful when looking back to evaluate the overall success of the educational experience and identify areas of revision. Such documentation is even more critical when you find yourself doing social justice workshops and structured conversations in between other priorities in your day. However, documentation is also a useful way to go about collaborating with others to enhance and share your work. If you find yourself, either now or in the future, working in an "office of one" or with few colleagues on your campus, having your process documented to share with others and solicit feedback can help you gain new insights. Frankly, we believe that the social justice education community can only benefit from sharing our work with one another. However, we can gain greater insights from our colleagues when we document our efforts using an intentional approach. That said, please document your process and consider sharing your process with others so that we all can learn and grow together in our practice.

At the start of this book, we shared Paul Wellstone's quote, "We all do better, when we all do better." Social inequality and related systems of privilege and oppression persist despite our best efforts to create a more socially just world. We hope this book helps you do better as a social justice educator so that we all can do better in a more socially just world. It is from this place that we have hope for our future.

Appendix: Annotated List of Activities

The following list provides brief descriptions of task-based activities referred to in the book, noting in which chapters they appear. As always, we urge you to carefully select the activities you use based on the context, student audience, and intended learning outcomes. Most of these activities have multiple variations that can be found online.

Let Me In (Chapter 5)
A symbolic activity where a group of students is asked to form a circle and instructed to prevent any other students from joining their group. The educator then proceeds to invite other students to attempt to join the group. Often, the activity illuminates common strategies used from in-groups and out-groups to navigate inclusion and exclusion.

Line Up (Chapter 4)
A symbolic activity where students are asked to form a line based on some criteria (e.g., where you were born). Educators can add a layer of complexity by also telling students they must do so without talking. The activity normally ends based on either a predetermined time limit or when students have completed the task.

Privilege Walk (Chapters 4, 9)
A simulation activity where the educator reads a series of prepared statements related to social identities or experiences and invites students to move forward or backward if the statement applies to them (e.g., I did not need to take out loans for school—step forward). The activity replicates social stratification based on students' social identity–based experiences.

Social Identity Salience Web (Chapter 9)
An introspective activity where students write out their social identities on a sheet of paper. The educator then invites students to eliminate (e.g., tear away, cross out) one or more of their social identities at a time until only one remains. The result leaves students with the social identity that is most significant or salient to them.

Social Identity Timeline (Chapter 4)
An introspective activity where students reflect on a specific social identity over time. Often students draw a horizontal line on a slip of paper, demarcate time periods based on age (e.g., 0–5 years) or relevant contexts (e.g., elementary school), and mark significant moments related to their social identity (e.g., when they first became aware of their race, a challenging moment related to race).

Social Identity Wheel (Chapters 4, 8)
An introspective activity that traditionally uses a handout with a wheel image with spokes for social identity categories (e.g., race) and space for students to write their social identity (e.g., Black). Additional prompts may be listed that invite students to reflect on their social identities. Prompts might include identifying which identities they think most and least about, the values they hold associated with their identities, or how their identities shape the way the view others and themselves.

Social Inequality Playing Card Simulation (Chapter 10)
A simulation activity where students are given a single playing card and told to hold it up so they cannot see the card's value but others can. The educator instructs students to interact with one another based on the value of the playing card (e.g., best treatment for aces, worst treatment for 2's). The activity continues long enough for students to interact with multiple people and for familiar group dynamics to arise during the activity.

References

Adams, M. (2016). Pedagogical foundations for social justice education. In M. Adams, L. A. Bell, D. J. Goodman, & K. Y. Joshi (Eds.), *Teaching for diversity and social justice* (3rd ed.) (pp. 27–53). Routledge.

Adams, M., Bell, L. A., Goodman, D. J., & Joshi, K. Y. (Eds.). (2016). *Teaching for diversity and social justice* (3rd ed.). Routledge.

Adams, M., Bell, L. A., & Griffin, P. (Eds.). (2007). *Teaching for diversity and social justice: A sourcebook* (2nd edition). Routledge.

Adams, M., Blumenfeld, W. J., Castañeda, C., Hackman, H. W., Peters, M. L., & Zúñiga, X. (Eds.). (2013). *Readings for diversity and social justice* (3rd ed.). Routledge.

Adichie, C. N. (2009, July). *The danger of a single story* [Video]. TED. https://www.ted.com/talks/chimamanda_adichie_the_danger_of_a_single_story/up-next

Ambrose, S. A., Bridges, M. W., DiPietro, M., Lovett, M. C., & Norman, M. K. (2010). *How learning works: Seven research-based principles for smart teaching.* Jossey-Bass.

American College Personnel Association (ACPA). (2019). *Annual convention program.* http://convention.myacpa.org/boston2019/wp-content/uploads/2019/02/ACPA19_Final_ProgramBook.pdf

American College Personnel Association (ACPA) & National Association of Student Personnel Administrators (NASPA). (2016, October). *ACPA/NASPA professional competencies rubrics.* https://www.naspa.org/images/uploads/main/ACPA_NASPA_Professional_Competency_Rubrics_Full.pdf

Amherst College Queer Resource Center. (n.d.). *Terms, definitions & labels.* https://www.amherst.edu/campuslife/our-community/queer-resource-center/terms-definitions

Bell, L. A. (2007). Theoretical foundations for social justice education. In M. Adams, L. A. Bell, & P. Griffin (Eds.), *Teaching for diversity and social justice: A sourcebook* (2nd ed.) (pp. 3–14). Routledge.

Bell, L. A., Goodman, D. J., & Ouellett, M. L. (2016). Design and facilitation. In M. Adams, L. A. Bell, D. J. Goodman, & K. Y. Joshi (Eds.), *Teaching for diversity and social justice* (3rd ed.) (pp. 55–93). Routledge.

Bell, L. A., Goodman, D. J., & Varghese, R. (2016). Critical self-knowledge for social justice educators. In M. Adams, L. A. Bell, D. J. Goodman, & K. Y. Joshi (Eds.), *Teaching for diversity and social justice* (3rd ed.) (pp. 397–418). Routledge.

Bell, L. A., & Griffin, P. (2007). Designing social justice education courses. In M. Adams, L. A. Bell, & P. Griffin (Eds.), *Teaching for diversity and social justice: A sourcebook* (2nd ed.) (pp. 67–87). Routledge.

Bell, L. A., Love, B. J., & Roberts, R. A. (2007). Racism and White privilege curriculum. In M. Adams, L. A. Bell, & P. Griffin (Eds.), *Teaching for diversity and social justice: A sourcebook* (2nd ed.) (pp. 15–33). Routledge.

Bennett, J. M. (2009). Transformative training: Designing programs for culture learning. In M. A. Moodian (Ed.), *Contemporary leadership and intercultural competence: Exploring the cross-cultural dynamics within organizations* (pp. 95–110). SAGE. http://dx.doi.org/10.4135/9781452274942.n8

Bennett, M. J. (2013). *Basic concepts of intercultural communication: Paradigms, principles, and practices* (2nd ed.). Intercultural Press.

Berastaín, P. (2017, August 31). *Should organizations use Latin@ or Latinx?* National Latin@ Network. https://enblog.nationallatinonetwork.org/should-organizations-use-latin-or-latinx/

Bonilla, J. F. (2011). Revisiting technology in the classroom: Critical reflections of a multiculturalist. *The Journal of Faculty Development, 25*(1), 28–35.

Bonilla, J. F., Lindeman, L. A., & Taylor, N. R. (2012). Educating for and assessing cultural competence. In K. A. Normal-Major & S. T. Gooden (Eds.), *Cultural competence for public administrators* (pp. 294–309). M. E. Sharpe.

Bowen, J. A. (2012). *Teaching naked: How moving technology out of your college classroom will improve student learning.* Jossey-Bass.

Bronfenbrenner, U. (1979). *The ecology of human development: Experiments by nature and design.* Harvard University Press.

Chessman, H. M., & Wayt, L. (2016, January 13). What are students demanding? *Higher Education Today.* https://www.higheredtoday.org/2016/01/13/what-are-students-demanding/

Collins, P. H. (2009). *Black feminist thought: Knowledge, consciousness, and the politics of empowerment.* Routledge.

Costa, K. (2020). *99 tips for creating simple and sustainable educational videos: A guide for online teachers and flipped classes.* Stylus.

Crenshaw, K. (1991). Mapping the margins: Intersectionality, identity politics, and violence against women of color. *Stanford Law Review, 43*(6), 1241–1299. https://www.jstor.org/stable/1229039

Domingue, A. D. (2016). Online and blended pedagogy in social justice education. In M. Adams, L. A. Bell, D. J. Goodman, & K. J. Yoshi (Eds.), *Teaching for diversity and social justice* (3rd ed., pp. 369–396). Routledge.

Espinosa, L., Chessman, H. M., & Wayt, L. (2016, March 8). Racial climate on campus: A survey of college presidents. *Higher Education Today.* https://www.highered today.org/2016/03/08/racial-climate-on-campus-a-survey-of-college-presidents/

Fanon, F. (1963). *The wretched of the earth.* Grove Atlantic.

Fanon, F. (1967). *Black skin, White masks.* Grove Atlantic.

Feagin, J. R., Vera, H., & Batur, P. (2001). *White racism* (2nd ed.). Routledge.

Fieldstadt, E., & Dilanian, K. (2019, August 5). *White nationalism-fueled violence is on the rise, but the FBI is slow to call it domestic terrorism.* NBC News. https://www.nbcnews.com/news/us-news/white-nationalism-fueled-violence-rise-fbi-slow-call-it-domestic-n1039206

Fink, L. D. (2013). *Creating significant learning experiences: An integrated approach to designing college courses.* Jossey-Bass.

Freire, P. (1998). *Teachers as cultural workers: Letters to those who dare teach* (D. Macedo, D. Koike, & A. Oliveira, Trans.). Westview Press.

Freire, P. (2000). *Pedagogy of the oppressed* (30th anniversary ed.). Bloomsbury.

Goodman, D. J. (1995). Difficult dialogues: Enhancing discussions about diversity. *College Teaching, 43*(2), 47–52. https://www.jstor.org/stable/27558705

Goodman, D. J. (2011). *Promoting diversity and social justice: Educating people from privileged groups* (2nd Edition). Routledge.

Goodman, D. J. (2013, February 5). Cultural competency for social justice. *Council for Social Justice Education Blog.* https://acpacsje.wordpress.com/2013/02/05/cultural-competency-for-social-justice-by-diane-j-goodman-ed-d/

Hafner, J. (2018, March 29). Police killings of Black men in the U.S. and what happened to the officers. *USA Today.* https://www.usatoday.com/story/news/nation-now/2018/03/29/police-killings-black-men-us-and-what-happened-officers/469467002/

Hardiman, R., Jackson, B. W., & Griffin, P. (2013). Conceptual foundations. In M. Adams, W. J. Blumenfeld, C. Castañeda, H. W. Hackman, M. L. Peters, & X. Zúñiga (Eds.) *Readings for diversity and social justice* (3rd ed.) (pp. 26–35). Routledge.

Hardiman, R., & Jackson, B. W. (1997). Conceptual foundations for social justice courses. In M. Adams, L. A. Bell, & P. Griffin (Eds.), *Teaching for diversity and social justice* (pp. 16–29). Routledge.

Hardiman, R., Jackson, B. W., & Griffin, P. (2007). Conceptual foundations for social justice courses. In M. Adams, L. A. Bell, & P. Griffin (Eds.), *Teaching for diversity and social justice* (2nd ed.) (pp. 35–66). Routledge.

Harro, B. (2013). Cycle of socialization. In M. Adams, W. J. Blumenfeld, C. Castañeda, H. W. Hackman, M. L. Peters, & X. Zúñiga (Eds.), *Readings for diversity and social justice* (3rd ed.) (pp. 45–52). Routledge.

hooks, b. (1994). *Teaching to transgress: Education as the practice of freedom.* Routledge.

Johnson, A. G. (2006). *Privilege, power, and difference* (2nd ed.). McGraw-Hill.

Jones, S. R., & Abes, E. S. (2013). *Identity development of college students: Advancing frameworks for multiple dimensions of identity.* Wiley.

Jordan, W. D. (2014). Historical origins of the one-drop racial rule in the united states. *Journal of Critical Mixed Race Studies, 1*(1), 98–132. https://escholarship.org/uc/item/91g761b3

Kearsley, G. (2005). *Online learning: Personal reflections on the transformation of education.* Educational Technology Publications.

Keeling, R. P. (Ed.). (2004). *Learning reconsidered: A campus-wide focus on the student experience.* NASPA/ACPA.

Keeling, R. P., Wall, A. F., Underhile, R., & Dungy, G. J. (2008). *Assessment reconsidered: Institutional effectiveness for student success.* International Center for Student Success and Institutional Accountability.

Kivel, P. (2013). *Living in the shadow of the cross: Understanding and resisting the power and privilege of Christian hegemony.* New Society Publishers.

Kolowich, S. (2015, November 20). Diversity training is in demand. Does it work? *The Chronicle of Higher Education.* http://chronicle.com/article/Diversity-Training-Is-in/234280

Lave, J., & Wenger, E. (1991). *Situated learning: Legitimate peripheral participation.* Cambridge University Press.

Maki, P. (2010). *Assessing for learning: Building a sustainable commitment across the institution* (2nd ed.). Stylus.

Matias, C. E. (2016). *Feeling White: Whiteness, emotionality, and education.* Sense Publishers.

McIntosh, P. (1989, July/August). White privilege: Unpacking the invisible knapsack. *Peace and Freedom Magazine,* 10–12. https://psychology.uhttp//www.mediainsight.org/PDFs/Journalism%202018/Americans_News_Media_Report_2018.pdfmbc.edu/files/2016/10/White-Privilege_McIntosh-1989.pdf

Media Insight Project. (2018, June). Americans and the new media: What they do—and don't—understand about each other. http://www.mediainsight.org/PDFs/Journalism%202018/Americans_News_Media_Report_2018.pdf

Montenegro, E., & Jankowski, N. A. (2017, January). *Equity and assessment: Moving towards culturally responsive assessment* (Occasional Paper No. 29). University of Illinois and Indiana University, National Institute for Learning Outcomes Assessment (NILOA). https://learningoutcomesassessment.org/documents/OccasionalPaper29.pdf

Nagda, B. A., Tropp, L. R., & Paluck, E. L. (2006). Looking back as we look ahead: Integrating research, theory and practice on intergroup relations. *Journal of Social Issues, 62*(3), 439–451. https://doi.org/10.1111/j.1540-4560.2006.00467.x

National Conference on Race and Ethnicity in American Higher Education (NCORE). (n.d.). *History and archive.* https://ncore.ou.edu/en/about/history-ncore/

National Conference on Race and Ethnicity in American Higher Education (NCORE). (2019). *NCORE 2019 program and resource guide.* https://ncore.ou.edu/media/filer_public/19/25/1925ee81-65eb-4582-89b4-d7fe33abe310/ncore_2019_program_guide_for_website.pdf

NewsOne Staff. (2015, November 4). News roundup: Half of Black millennials know a police brutality victim . . . and more. *Chicago Defender.* Available from NewsBank: Access World News. https://newsone.com/3238259/roundup-half-of-black-millennials-know-police-brutality-victim/

Nilson, L. B. (2010). *Teaching at its best: A research-based resource for college instructors* (3rd ed.). Jossey Bass.

Nodjimbadem, K. (2017, July 27). The long, painful history of police brutality in the U.S. *Smithsonian Magazine.* https://www.smithsonianmag.com/smithsonian-institution/long-painful-history-police-brutality-in-the-us-180964098/

Obear, K. (2007). Navigating triggering events: Critical skills for facilitating difficult dialogues. *The Diversity Factor, 15*(3), 23–29.

Ordover, N. (2003). *American eugenics: Race, queer anatomy, and the science of nationalism.* University of Minnesota Press. https://www.jstor.org/stable/10.5749/j.ctttt7tz

Perrin, A., & Anderson M. (2019, April 10). *Share of U.S. adults using social media, including Facebook, is mostly unchanged since 2018.* Pew Research Center. https://www.pewresearch.org/fact-tank/2019/04/10/share-of-u-s-adults-using-social-media-including-facebook-is-mostly-unchanged-since-2018/

Pope, R. L., & Reynolds, A. L. (1997). Student affairs core competencies: Integrating multicultural awareness, knowledge, and skills. *Journal of College Student Development, 38*(3), 266–277.

Pope, R. L., Reynolds, A. L. & Mueller, J. A. (2019). *Multicultural competence in student affairs: Advancing social justice and inclusion* (2nd ed.). Jossey-Bass.

Reif, L. R. (2013, September 26). Online learning will make college cheaper. It will also make it better. *Time, 182*(15), 54–55. https://nation.time.com/2013/09/26/online-learning-will-make-college-cheaper-it-will-also-make-it-better/

Rhodes, T. L. (2010). *Assessing outcomes and improving achievement: Tips and tools for using rubrics.* Association of American Colleges and Universities.

Rudestam, K. E., & Schoenholtz-Read, J. (2010). *Handbook of online learning* (2nd ed.). SAGE.

Stephenson, J. (2001). *Teaching and learning online: Pedagogies for new technologies.* Routledge.

Sue, D. W. (2001). Multidimensional facets of cultural competence. *The Counseling Psychologist, 29*(6), 790–821. https://doi.org/10.1177/0011000001296002

Sue, D. W., Bernier, J. E., Durran, A., Feinberg, L., Pedersen, P., Smith, E. J., & Vasquez-Nuttall, E. (1982). Position paper: Cross-cultural counseling competencies. *The Counseling Psychologist, 10*(20), 45–52. https://doi.org/10.1177/0011000082102008

Suskie, L. (2009). *Assessing student learning: A common sense guide* (2nd ed.). Jossey-Bass.

Tajfel, H., & Turner, J. C. (1979). An integrative theory of intergroup conflict. In W. G. Austin & S. Worchel (Eds.), *The social psychology of intergroup relations* (pp. 33–47). Brooks/Cole.

Tatum, B. D. (1994). Teaching White students about racism: The search for White allies and the restoration of hope. *Teacher's College Record, 95*(4), 462–476.

Tervalon, M., & Murray-Garcia, J. (1998). Cultural humility versus cultural competence: A critical distinction in defining physician training outcomes in multicultural education. *Journal of Health Care for the Poor and Undeserved, 9*(2), 117–125. http://doi.org/10.1353/hpu.2010.0233

Tharp, D. S. (2015, November). *A proposed framework for social justice education workshop design.* Paper presented at the Annual Association for the Study of Higher Education Conference, Denver, CO.

Tharp, D. S. (2017). Imagining flipped workshops: Considerations for designing online modules for social justice education workshops. *Multicultural Perspectives, 19*(3), 178–184. https://doi.org/10.1080/15210960.2017.1335081

Tinker, B. (2004). *LARA: Engaging controversy with a non-violent, transformative response* [Workshop handout available by request by Love Makes a Family, Inc.].

Torres, V. (2011). Perspectives on identity development. In J. H. Schuh, S. R. Jones, S. R. Harper, & Associates (Eds.), *Student services: A handbook for the profession* (5th ed.) (pp. 187–206). Jossey-Bass.

Torres, V., Howard-Hamilton, M. F., & Cooper, D. L. (2003). Identity development of diverse populations: Implications for teaching and administration in higher education. *ASHE-ERIC Higher Education Report, 26*(6). Jossey-Bass.

Vygotsky, L. S. (1978). *Mind in society: The development of higher psychological processes.* Harvard University Press.

Wah, L. M. (2004). *The art of mindful facilitation.* Stirfry Seminars and Consulting.

Walvoord, B. E. (2010). *Assessment clear and simple: A practical guide for institutions, departments, and general education* (2nd ed.). Jossey-Bass.

Watt, S. K. (2015). Privileged identity exploration (PIE) model revisited: Strengthening skills for engaging difference. In S. K. Watt (Ed.), *Designing transformative multicultural initiatives: Theoretical foundations, practical applications, and facilitator considerations* (pp. 40–57). Stylus.

Weinmeyer, R. (2014, November). The decriminalization of sodomy in the United States. *American Medical Association Journal of Ethics.* https://journalofethics.ama-assn.org/article/decriminalization-sodomy-united-states/2014-11

Winant, H. (1997). Behind blue eyes: Whiteness and contemporary U.S. racial politics. In M. Fine, L. Weis, L. C. Powell, & L. M. Wong (Eds.), *Off White: Readings on race, power, and society* (pp. 40–53). Routledge.

Winfield, A. G. (2007). *Eugenics and education in America: Institutionalized racism and the implications of history, ideology, and memory.* Peter Lang.

Winkelmes, M., Boye, A., & Tapp, S. (Eds). (2019). *Transparent design in higher education teaching and leadership: A guide to implementing the transparency framework institution-wide to improve learning and retention.* Stylus.

Wise, T., & Case, K. A. (2013). Pedagogy for the privileged: Addressing inequality and injustice without shame or blame. In K. A. Case (Ed.), *Deconstructing privilege: Teaching and learning as allies in the classroom* (pp. 17–33). Routledge.

Zúñiga, X., Nagda, B. A., Chesler, M., & Cytron-Walker, A. (2007). Intergroup dialogues in higher education: Meaningful learning about social justice. *ASHE Higher Education Report Series, 32*(4), 1–28.

Index